RESILIENCE

BOOKS IN THE LIBRARY FUTURES SERIES

Resilience, by Rebekkah Smith Aldrich

Anonymity (forthcoming), by Alison Macrina and Talya Cooper

Blockchain (forthcoming), by Susan Alman and Sandra Hirsh

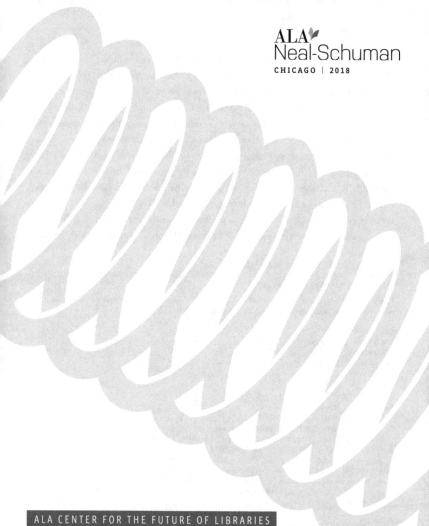

ALA Neal-Schuman
CHICAGO | 2018

ALA CENTER FOR THE FUTURE OF LIBRARIES

RESILIENCE

REBEKKAH SMITH ALDRICH

LIBRARY FUTURES ②

REBEKKAH SMITH ALDRICH is a passionate advocate for public libraries because she knows that libraries can change the world. She currently serves as the coordinator for library sustainability at the Mid-Hudson Library System (New York), where she daily assists sixty-six public libraries in the areas of leadership, funding, and facilities. Aldrich is the sustainability columnist for *Library Journal*, the author of the *Handbook for New Public Library Directors in New York State*, coauthor of the *Handbook for Public Library Trustees of New York State*, and author of *Sustainable Thinking* from the American Library Association. She was a founding member of both the American Library Association's Sustainability Roundtable and the New York Library Association's Sustainability Initiative. Rebekkah is proud of her work to help pass the 2015 "ALA Resolution on the Importance of Sustainable Libraries." Named a *Library Journal* Mover & Shaker, Aldrich is a frequent national presenter on the topic of leading libraries forward in smart, practical, and effective ways.

ISBNs
978-0-8389-1634-6 (paper)
978-0-8389-1754-1 (PDF)
978-0-8389-1753-4 (ePub)
978-0-8389-1755-8 (Kindle)

Library of Congress Cataloging-in-Publication Data

Names: Aldrich, Rebekkah Smith. | Center for the Future of Libraries.
Title: Resilience / Rebekkah Smith Aldrich.
Description: Chicago : ALA Neal-Schuman, an imprint of the American Library Association, 2018. | Series: Library Futures series | At head of title: Center for the Future of Libraries.
Identifiers: LCCN 2018009907 | ISBN 9780838916346 (print : alk. paper) | ISBN 9780838917534 (epub : alk. paper) | ISBN 9780838917541 (pdf : alk. paper) | ISBN 9780838917558 (kindle : alk. paper)
Subjects: LCSH: Libraries and community. | Libraries and society. | Library planning. | Emergency management—Planning. | Sustainability. | Libraries and community—United States—Case studies.
Classification: LCC Z716.4 A445 2018 | DDC 021.2—dc23 LC record available at https://lccn.loc.gov/2018009907

Cover design by Kimberly Thornton. Composition by Alejandra Diaz in the Adobe Garamond Pro, Vista Sans and Vista Slab typefaces.

♾ This paper meets the requirements of ANSI/NISO Z39.48–1992 (Permanence of Paper).

Printed in the United States of America
22 21 20 19 18   5 4 3 2 1

ALA Neal-Schuman purchases fund advocacy, awareness, and accreditation programs for library professionals worldwide.

CONTENTS

FOREWORD

BY MIGUEL A. FIGUEROA
Center for the Future of Libraries
American Library Association

RESILIENCE HAS BECOME ONE OF THOSE WORDS APPLIED expediently as a salve for any one of a number of issues in today's society. Students and children need to develop grit and resilience to succeed in an increasingly competitive environment. Displaced communities are praised for their resilience as neighborhoods flood and electrical grids fail. Employees need to be resilient to changing demands and reduced resources.

If today's concept of resilience often seems to shift the burden to the individual or creates a top-down approach, how does it fit into a profession like librarianship whose past and future are testament to the collective powers of community?

In *Resilience*, Rebekkah Smith Aldrich re-centers the concept to show its alignment with our profession's values and its usefulness for guiding our future roles in communities. In these times of disruption and change, a more reflective understanding of resilience inspires us to think more deeply about our enduring work and our commitment to diversity, education, engagement, equitable access, preservation, service to the public good, and social responsibility. It also provides us with a new framework for achieving these goals with greater urgency and efficiency.

Rebekkah begins by demonstrating how resilience has become a central trend in a world of disruptions. To the excellent sources she references, I will highlight the work of UN-Habitat, the United Nations program that promotes socially and environmentally sustainable development and the achievement of adequate shelter for all. UN-Habitat identifies resilience as a key theme in the pursuit of better urban futures and defines it as "the ability of human settlements to withstand and to recover quickly from any plausible hazards . . . not only . . . reducing risks and damage from disasters . . . but also the ability to quickly bounce back to a stable state."[1] UN-Habitat's "Ten Essentials" pursue an ongoing system of empowerment for communities—at least half for building resilience align with many libraries' goals and values for their communities.[2]

Rebekkah's compelling vision outlined in "Resilience in Libraries" roots our resilience work in our role as community conveners, bringing people together with information, with each other, and with other organizations and institutions. She helps us see that libraries can restore a vision for resilience that empowers the individual and the collective.

"From the Field" considers how a resilience strategy aligns with what truly great libraries have done and will continue to do. Rebekkah looks at libraries' resilience strategies in response to disruptions, in the planning of our buildings and services, in our engagement with communities, and in our roles as educators, preparing individuals with the skills to live their best lives.

In "For the Future," Rebekkah points to the urgent need for resilience strategies in our communities and the ways that libraries can work to not only make our own organizations resilient to disruptions, but also to create a system of resilience that benefits all members of the community.

Because of Rebekkah's work—and the work of colleagues across our profession, including the American Library Association's Sustainability Roundtable[3]—resilience was among the first trends included in the Center for the Future of Libraries' trend collection.[4] Reading *Resilience*, I am recommitted to the ways that resilience, pursuing an inclusive framework for responding to disruption and empowering all members of a community, aligns with our professional values and the usefulness it can have for shaping the future of libraries.

---

1. https://unhabitat.org/urban-themes/resilience/.
2. Ibid.
3. www.ala.org/rt/sustainrt.
4. www.ala.org/tools/future/trends.

UNDERSTANDING RESILIENCE

WE LIVE IN UNCERTAIN TIMES.

Uncertainty on many fronts—political, economic, technological, environmental—confronts our everyday lives and our planning for the future. With increased access to data, news, and opinion, the variations on the themes of our day are complicated, often obscuring our path forward as communities. As a community leader, cultivating a clear vision for the future must take into account the need for increased resiliency.

Resilience, by definition, is a capacity that enables people, places, and systems to **survive, adapt, and thrive**.[1] Resilience is multifaceted: it can refer to infrastructure, individuals, environmental or economic systems, and organizations.

Resilience can be naturally built in (as in healthy ecosystems) or be deliberately developed (as in sustainable building designs). In an increasingly **complex and interconnected** world, we are in the race of our lives to plan further and

---

1. https://www.rockefellerfoundation.org/blog/three-trends-shaping-future-food/.

further ahead as the severity and frequency of environmental, social, and economic disruptions continue to intensify.

It is easy to have blinders on. It is easy to focus on immediate issues of concern, such as the price of e-books, the challenges of managing new staff who are from a different generation than yours, the difficulties associated with being managed by someone from a different generation than yours, or the fact that the air conditioning on the second floor of the library doesn't ever seem to work right. It is challenging to keep our eyes focused on what is going on around us, outside the library, and to **synthesize the implications** of changes in our world for our library and community.

But that is part of the work: **situational awareness**.

In the military, officers will ask their soldiers for a "sitrep," a report on the current situation in a particular area. Officers then collate that data from various areas to course-correct their plans to ensure that they have the latest intel to base decisions on. To provide a sitrep, soldiers have to be constantly vigilant, and to maintain that vigilance, they cultivate a high level of *situational awareness.*

Situational awareness today reveals amplified disruption on just about every front—political, economic, technological, environmental, and societal.

SITUATIONAL AWARENESS

Situational awareness is the ability to identify, process, and comprehend the critical information about what is happening with regard to the mission. More simply, it's knowing what is going on around you. ("Team Coordination Training Student Guide," United States Coast Guard)

I use the phrase *amplified disruption* deliberately. There has always been, and always will be, disruption. However, disruption in the modern world is amplified by a 24/7 news cycle and the content- and engagement-hungry social media landscape. Reaction time is on a fast cycle, causing people to say, do, and think things in ways they did not when they got their serving of the day's news from one of three television channels or two newspapers thirty years ago.

The media's influence on our experience today exacerbates the challenges we face. Media outlets are growing increasingly desperate to hold on to our attention. They stoop to new lows, amplifying what has always been a profitable tactic: keeping us scared. The media manipulate our worldview to better profit from sensationalistic political disagreements, criminal altercations, and international incidents. This strategy creates a vicious cycle that deepens the divide between segments of our society, decreasing the likelihood that we will work together to address the challenges and opportunities that we are all faced with.

DISRUPTION IN OUR WORLD

Political **disruption** can be felt locally and internationally. Outrageous displays between world leaders who bait each other to push the button, rollbacks of decades-old environmental and tax policies that destabilize our future, partisan politicians who cannot work across the aisle for the betterment of those they serve—all these disrupt the work that needs to be done on behalf of ourselves. We suffer through the hackneyed national political sphere—amplified in the age of cable news, niche online publications, Twitter, and discussion boards—where various players jockey for position, pander to the camera, and search for the sound bite or the retweetable burn that will launch them into, or keep them in, the spotlight. We watch, internationally, as governments are overthrown, and in some cases, marginalized, creating chaos and uncertainty, and we wonder what will happen next.

Economic **disruption** is happening at a faster and faster pace, for better or for worse. From recession, the loss of manufacturing jobs, and the antitax movement to the sharing economy on the Internet, cryptocurrencies, emerging markets, and the Fourth Industrial Revolution—change is happening, and it is happening fast. Our current economy is a delicate thing, changing some industries seemingly overnight, leaving larger and larger swaths of people out of the arena of economic security and leveraging others' failure for gain. It is a rapidly moving, twisting, changing "thing" that can make some people fabulously wealthy while the vast majority are left fighting for scraps.

Technological **disruption** is a favorite topic of libraries and the public. Today it is the impact of livecasting your interaction with a police officer, and of artificially intelligent video editing that allows anyone to put words in your mouth if you've been videotaped.[2] Tomorrow? Who knows! Tech can disrupt—for better or for worse—a variety of sectors: the economy, society, politics. Paying attention to these disruptions is essential for understanding the modern world and participating in it. Basic needs are affected by technology when governments work to harness the power of tech to deliver services that impact health care, housing, and food. Basic needs are impacted by technology when hackers use programs such as ransomware to hold hostage our personal information or when supposedly secure systems are hacked, releasing sensitive information that can change the landscape overnight. It's not enough for the technological elite to follow the changes shaped by tech; this is a topic that impacts us all.

---

2. Jennifer Langston, "Lip-Syncing Obama: New Tools Turn Audio Clips into Realistic Video," *UW News*, July 11, 2017, www.washington.edu/news/2017/07/11/lip-syncing-obama-new-tools-turn-audio-clips-into-realistic-video/.

Environmental **disruption** is perhaps the most brutal and unforgiving disruption of all. It impacts our survivability on this planet. Climate change brought on by decisions made by humans over hundreds of years is now resulting in severe weather patterns that bring on life-threatening floods, droughts, fires, depletion of natural resources, and dangerous air that we all breathe. Your views may vary on how climate change is impacting your locality, but there is no doubt that food insecurity and access to fresh air, water, and livable places are human issues, not just local issues.

Social **disruption** is inevitable in the face of the massive disturbances just listed, and this area of disruption exacerbates all the others: political, economic, technological, and environmental. When people are pitted against each other for access to seemingly limited resources, when lobbyists purposefully undermine actual dialogue on issues, when others gain from one group's disagreement with another group, we are fractured as a society. Social disruption can take many forms—gun violence, orphaned seniors, racism, terrorism, opioid abuse, and protest marches. As Martin Luther King Jr. said, "A riot is the language of the unheard."[3]

We are in societal silos, clinging to long-held beliefs, lashing out at one another, disparaging differences of opinion to such a heated degree that violence is breaking out. Are there justified grievances? Absolutely. Is there a civil dialogue that informs change and growth? Not much. When our government is close to non-functioning and civic leadership is weakened by the toxicity of the political sphere, **the social fabric of our communities becomes frayed and is weakened**.

Disruption can have positive impacts as well as negative impacts and resilience can play just as large a role in that construct. A good example of the balance between good and bad disruption is nowhere more evident

---

3. https://www.cbsnews.com/news/mlk-a-riot-is-the-language-of-the-unheard/.

than in the advent of the Internet. While many focus on the ills of the Internet—loss of privacy, degradation of communication skills, criminal enterprises—the Internet has empowered economic innovation, creative problem-solving, and increased access to information in ways that we could not have imagined thirty, twenty, or even ten years ago. Finding opportunity in the face of disruption is not always an evil act. It can be beautiful, inspiring, and hopeful—helping our neighbors, solving problems, and providing new paths to understanding in the analog world. The key to our success will lie in our attitude about change and disruption. A resilient mindset will require that we embrace curiosity, pragmatism, and fast-cycle threat assessment.

THE ROLES OF GOVERNMENT AND NET STATES

Resilience planning by governments at every level—national, state, county, and local—is most prominently focused on addressing natural disasters and the impacts of climate change, largely due to the acute nature of severe weather events such as Hurricane Katrina (2005), Hurricane Sandy (aka Superstorm Sandy) (2012), and Hurricane Maria (2017). The year 2017 was the most expensive severe weather year in recorded history,[4] and according to the Intergovernmental Panel on Climate Change's *Fourth Assessment Report* (IPCC, 2007),[5] "confidence has increased that some weather events and extremes will become more frequent, more widespread or more intense during the 21st century."

This has certainly been borne out in recent years with historic droughts, heat waves, rainfall, wildfires, hurricanes, and coastal flooding the likes of which we have not seen in our lifetimes.

---

4. https://www.washingtonpost.com/news/energy-environment/wp/2018/01/08/hurricanes-wildfires-made-2017-the -most-costly-u-s-disaster-year-on-record/?utm_term=.cb7d9eaf9cd0.
5. https://www.ipcc.ch/publications_and_data/ar4/wg2/en/spmsspm-c-15-magnitudes-of.html.

Municipalities and county and state governments have and are developing resiliency plans that address the issues they are confronted with on the environmental front. For areas prone to flooding and hurricanes, their plans will include evacuation protocols, redundancy plans for electrical grids, the deployment of solar solutions to keep critical services going, storm water runoff reduction and management plans, and team-building exercises for the first responder community. In California's plan you will find a comprehensive approach to implementing drought resilience measures and dealing with land and forest management issues to combat the deadly increase in wildfires they have been contending with.

In a critical turn of events, government resilience planning at the state and local levels is evolving from plans that focused on response and recovery after a disaster occurs to **mitigation and adaptation techniques** that will help minimize risk *before* an extreme weather or climate event occurs. There is a rise in decentralized approaches to dealing with risk mitigation and response, given a national political climate which is threatening to derail progress. Local primacy in planning is paramount, not only because it is the most effective path to actually implementing a plan, but because of the loss of faith in our national leadership to do what is best for our country.

At the federal level, the word "resilience" has been co-opted in an attempt to deny climate change as the reason why we are all scrambling to adapt to the vulnerabilities generated by decades of abuse of our planet. In early 2017 the Trump administration issued a memo to employees of the Natural Resources Conservation Service, which is part of the U.S. Department of Agriculture. The memo directs employees to avoid the term "climate change" and to instead use the term "weather extremes." Instead of "climate change adaptation," the recommended terms include "resilience to weather extremes." Rather than "reducing greenhouse gases," the e-mails suggest: "build soil organic matter, increase nutrient use efficiency."[6]

The obfuscation of the phrase "climate change" and the attempt to shift the focus onto individual, reactive resiliency is a **dangerous and foolish** move that will only exacerbate the damage we are contending with in the face of climate change. Without attention to continued mitigation efforts alongside disaster preparedness and post-event recovery planning, we are only adding to the level of devastation that humanity will face in the coming years.

Seven years after the IPCC's *Fourth Assessment Report*, they issued their *Fifth Assessment Report: Climate Change 2014: Impacts, Adaptation, and Vulnerability*.[7] This report is important for several reasons, not the least of which is that it is the first time we see this body actively shift the narrative from "*saving* the planet" to "*surviving* the planet."

Like scenes out of dystopian science fiction novels and disaster movies, the report lays out the **harsh reality** of what is coming:

- "Until mid-century, projected climate change will impact human health mainly by exacerbating health problems that already exist (*very high confidence*)."
- "Due to sea level rise projected throughout the 21st century and beyond, coastal systems and low-lying areas will increasingly experience adverse impacts such as submergence, coastal flooding, and coastal erosion (*very high confidence*)."
- "Climate change over the 21st century is projected to reduce renewable surface water and groundwater resources significantly in most dry subtropical regions (*robust evidence, high agreement*)."

---

6. www.cnn.com/2017/08/08/politics/usda-climate-change/index.html.

7. https://www.ipcc.ch/pdf/assessment-report/ar5/wg2/ar5_wgII_spm_en.pdf.

- "All aspects of food security are potentially affected by climate change, including food access, utilization, and price stability (*high confidence*)."
- "Climate change can indirectly increase risks of violent conflicts in the form of civil war and inter-group violence by amplifying well-documented drivers of these conflicts such as poverty and economic shocks (*medium confidence*)."

The survivability of our natural world is greatly influenced by non-environmental factors. Unfortunately, disasters that test the resilience of a community can take many forms, and there is a growing need to broaden our definitions of resilience planning in the face of various types of disruptions that can lead to disasters. In addition to the severe weather and climate extremes that we are contending with, there is an increased need to apply resilience strategies in the context of an overall rise in social and economic disruptions:

- Civil unrest (e.g., Occupy Wall Street, Ferguson, MO, Dakota Access Pipeline protests, Charlottesville, VA)
- "Active shooter" events or "mass casualty shootings" (e.g., Sandy Hook Elementary School, Pulse Nightclub, Las Vegas massacre, Marjory Stoneman Douglas High School)
- Economic disparity predictions (e.g., gender gap in salaries; universal basic income plans)
- Food insecurity (e.g., Mississippi, Alabama)
- Black hat hacking/cyberterrorism incidents (e.g., 2016 presidential election, WannaCry ransomware, Equifax breach)

The trajectories of these disasters are on the rise, just as environmental disasters are. For example, the Federal Bureau of Investigation reports that the annual number of active shooter events has increased dramatically over the past fifteen years, from one incident in 2000 to twenty in 2016.[8] In addition, the number of people killed or injured annually in active shooter incidents has increased by more than 100 percent between 2000 and 2015.[9] In 2018 there has been, on average, one school shooting a week so far.[10]

Black hat hacking or cyberterrorism (e.g., identity theft, DDoS (distributed denial-of-service) attacks, ransomware, zero-day exploits) is predicted to become the next massive economic, and possibly political, disaster. The growing wave of cybercrime has caused economic damage—in the form of stolen money, theft of intellectual property, theft of personal and financial data, lost productivity, and reputation destruction and restoration—that is difficult to estimate. The most recent estimates put the global cost at $600 billion, about 0.8 percent of the GDP. This is an enormous jump from $445 billion in 2014.[11] By 2021 the costs are expected to be in the trillions. Experts attribute the predicted increase to what they have dubbed a **"hackerpocalypse"**: a dramatic increase in cybercrime sponsored by hostile nation-states and hacking activities by organized criminal gangs. Cyber criminals, possibly state-sponsored, are under investigation for tampering with the 2016 presidential election, a good lesson that cybercrime has not only economic but political and social implications as well.

---

8. https://www.fbi.gov/file-repository/activeshooter_incidents_2001-2016.pdf/view.

9. https://ovc.ncjrs.gov/ncvrw2017/images/en_artwork/Fact_Sheets/2017NCVRW_MassShootings_508.pdf.

10. https://www.cnn.com/2018/03/02/us/school-shootings-2018-list-trnd/index.html.

11. https://www.cnbc.com/2018/02/22/cybercrime-pandemic-may-have-cost-the-world-600-billion-last-year.html.

> We believe that data is the phenomenon of our time. It is the world's new natural resource. It is the new basis of competitive advantage, and it is transforming every profession and industry. If all of this is true—even inevitable—then cybercrime, by definition, is the greatest threat to every profession, every industry, every company in the world.
>
> **Ginni Rometty, chairman, president, CEO, IBM Corp.**[12]

Predictions and data trends show a clear line to **more chaos**, violence, and potential devastation in our future. The work today should be to bring the world together to find solutions, however fractured and distracted we may be due to powerful forces in politics, business, and the media. Government is increasingly dismissed as dysfunctional, and corporations and citizens are taking matters into their own hands. For example, the rise of "net states," digital non-state actors that advance "belief-driven agendas that they pursue separate from, and at times, above, the law,"[13] is indicative of groups of people—sometimes in the form of corporations (Google, Facebook) and sometimes as hacktivist collectives (Anonymous, Wikileaks)—that are **no longer waiting** for traditional leaders or for what they perceive as out-of-date approaches to tell them what to do.

The decentralization of action, activism, and agitation greatly changes the landscape of what can happen, but it is clear that **what was predictable in the past is no longer so.**

Politicians and captains of industry profit from a fractured and siloed society. Factioned communities are polarized on issues and candidates

---

12. https://www.forbes.com/sites/stevemorgan/2015/11/24/ibms-ceo-on-hackers-cyber-crime-is-the-greatest -threat-to-every-company-in-the-world/.
13. https://www.wired.com/story/net-states-rule-the-world-we-need-to-recognize-their-power/.

and are unable to come together to mount a resistance against corporations that are profiting off of our natural resources and our fears about the future. Entrenchment is the word of the day: people are digging in on their perceptions of the world around them, fighting an often-unknown enemy because they feel threatened, and this in turn is distracting communities from the real work that needs to be done. This, at times, leaves a leadership vacuum that nontraditional leaders—be they a positive or negative force—can step in to.

A CULTURE OF RESILIENCE

Disaster risk is not shared equally by a population. There are those in our communities who are more vulnerable than others, since social, physical, economic, and environmental factors can contribute to greater exposure to disruption and disasters and hinder individuals' ability to recover in the aftermath of such events. People with fewer financial and social resources struggle to recover more than their more affluent and better-connected peers. The same goes for communities: communities with large concentrations of vulnerable people will be less resilient in the face of environmental, social, and economic disruptions and slower to bounce back.

The IPCC report points out that there are different levels of vulnerability in communities in the face of climate change-related disasters, thanks to non-climatic factors and inequalities in our society:

> Uncertainties about future vulnerability, exposure, and responses of interlinked human and natural systems are large. This motivates exploration of a wide range of socioeconomic futures in assessments of risks. Understanding future vulnerability, exposure, and response

capacity of interlinked human and natural systems is challenging
due to the number of *interacting social, economic, and cultural factors*,
which have been incompletely considered to date. These factors
include wealth and its distribution across society, demographics,
migration, *access to technology and information*, employment patterns, the quality of adaptive responses, societal values, governance
structures, and institutions to resolve conflicts.[14]

Disruption does not always mean disaster. Disasters occur as a result
of the effects of a hazardous event on a vulnerable community. "Vulnerability is place-based and context-specific."[15] That context can be
time-sensitive as well. There are immediate disasters (e.g., tornados
and hurricanes), but there are also slow-moving disasters that occur
due to chronic stressors that weaken the fabric of a community (e.g.,
unemployment, crime, food shortages).

Civil unrest is usually triggered by a specific event, but often the true
root of the unrest can be traced to an **ongoing frustration** with disparate
and unjust socioeconomic conditions. "Risk exposure can be separated
into two levels," says Cindy Lambdin, a health care coordinator with
the San Francisco Department of Public Health. "The first is the risk
posed by persistent disruption to the availability of items such as food
or medication or access to transportation, businesses, or one's residence.
The second is the risk of physical injuries and emotional trauma that
civil unrest can cause during the acute event." In *Exploring Disaster
Risk Reduction through Community-Level Approaches to Promote Healthy
Outcomes,* a report of the proceedings of the 2016 Preparedness Summit,
a national conference on public health preparedness, Lambdin went

14. https://www.ipcc.ch/pdf/assessment-report/ar5/wg2/ar5_wgII_spm_en.pdf.
15. https://www.nap.edu/read/18996/chapter/6#53.

on to suggest that a lack of education, a lack of mobility, poor coping skills, mental and behavioral health issues, weak family structures, and unemployment may all be individual vulnerabilities that contribute to civil unrest.[16]

We cannot respond our way out of disasters.

Mollie Mahany, public health advisor, Centers for Disease Control and Prevention[17]

In 1863 President Abraham Lincoln signed a congressional charter to form the National Academy of Sciences, citing the government's urgent need for an *independent* adviser on scientific matters. In a 2012 report from the National Academies, *Disaster Resilience: A National Imperative,* the respected institute stated: "Developing a *culture of resilience* would bolster support for preparedness and response, and would also enable better anticipation of disasters and their consequences, enhancing the ability to recover more quickly and strongly. Resilient communities would plan and build in ways that would reduce disaster losses, rather than waiting for a disaster to occur and paying for it afterward" (italics added).[18]

Holistic, community-based risk-reduction strategies can be used to **prevent and reduce exposure** and vulnerability to disasters, increase the readiness for response and recovery, and therefore strengthen resilience in a community.

---

16. https://www.nap.edu/read/23600/chapter/1#6.

17. https://www.nap.edu/read/23600/chapter/1#2.

18. *Disaster Resilience—A National Imperative* (Summary), National Academies (Washington, DC: National Academies Press, 2012), available from www.nap.edu/html/13457/13457_summary.pdf.

The Sendai Framework outlines four priorities for action to prevent new and reduce existing disaster risks:

(i) Understanding disaster risk

(ii) Strengthening disaster risk governance to manage disaster risk

(iii) Investing in disaster reduction for resilience

(iv) Enhancing disaster preparedness for effective response, and to "Build Back Better" in the course of recovery, rehabilitation, and reconstruction

The United Nations' Sendai Framework for Disaster Risk Reduction (2015–2030)[19] followed the National Academies report and takes an important perspective on resilience planning, shifting the emphasis from disaster management (where the focus is primarily on recovery after the disaster) to disaster risk management, or disaster risk reduction. **Disaster risk reduction** is a systematic approach to identifying, assessing, and reducing the risks of disaster. It aims to reduce socioeconomic vulnerabilities to disaster, as well as deal with the environmental and other hazards that trigger them.

As you read through the multitude of reports studying resilience strategies around the world, from government agencies in the United States to the United Nations, the World Health Organization, and nongovernmental organizations, the principal need for **"social cohesion"** is seen over and over again.

19. www.unisdr.org/we/inform/publications/43291.

> Social cohesion is defined as the willingness of members of a society to cooperate with each other in order to survive and prosper. Willingness to cooperate means they freely choose to form partnerships and have a reasonable chance of realizing goals, because others are willing to cooperate and share the fruits of their endeavors equitably.
>
> **Dick Stanley**[20]

Social cohesion can be visualized as "the social fabric." When knit tightly together, the social fabric is what holds us together and will increase our chances of survival and resilience in the face of disruption. Ongoing work to strengthen that fabric by promoting **understanding**, **respect**, **empathy**, and **interconnectedness** is one of the most critical aspects of both pre- and post-disaster resilience planning.

Social cohesion comes from truly living as a community, not just from proximity in a town or a neighborhood, but as actual neighbors who are working together to create a better place in the world to **live, love, and learn**. Social cohesion requires "**cultural competence**": "a set of congruent behaviors, attitudes, and policies that come together in a system, agency, or among professionals and enables effective work in cross-cultural situations."[21] Cultural competence is the ability to interact effectively with people of different cultures, helping to ensure that the needs of all community members are addressed.

This thread runs through all of the international and national reports, directives, programs, and philosophies on this subject: the development of *socially cohesive, sustainable communities* is essential to planning for resilience.

---

20. Dick Stanley, "What Do We Know about Social Cohesion: The Research Perspective of the Federal Government's Social Cohesion Research Network," *The Canadian Journal of Sociology* 28, no. 1, special issue (Winter 2003): 5–17.
21. L. M. Anderson, S. C. Scrimshaw, M. T. Fullilove J. E. Fielding, and J. Normand, Task Force on Community Preventive Services, "Culturally Competent Healthcare Systems: A Systematic Review," *American Journal of Preventive Medicine* 2003; 24(3S): 68–79, www.thecommunityguide.org/social/soc-AJPM-evrev-healthcare-systems.pdf.

How we define and measure a "sustainable community" is getting a lot of help from both the United Nations' Sustainable Development Goals and the STAR Community Index.

The Sustainable Development Goals (SDGs), otherwise known as the Global Goals, are a universal call to action to end poverty, protect the planet, and ensure that all people enjoy peace and prosperity (see figure 1):

1. No poverty
2. Zero hunger
3. Good health and well-being
4. Quality education
5. Gender equality
6. Clean water and sanitation
7. Affordable and clean energy
8. Decent work and economic growth
9. Industry, innovation, and infrastructure
10. Reduced inequalities
11. Sustainable cities and communities
12. Responsible consumption and production
13. Climate action
14. Life below water
15. Life on land
16. Peace, justice, and strong institutions
17. Partnerships for the goals

The SDGs provide global guidance for local decision-making. As each layer of government and each local institution makes choices about their priorities, their alignment with these goals strengthens the global community's ability to thrive.

FIGURE 1 ─────────────────────────────

United Nations Sustainable Development Goals

While the SDGs provide top-level compass settings, as we get closer to the local level we can see that the development of sustainable communities is integral to resilience planning. The Sustainability Tools for Assessing and Rating Communities (STAR) Community Index is an attempt to develop **a single, national, consensus-based framework for sustainability.** Among the guiding principles for developing the index are the following:

- Think and act systemically
- Instill resilience
- Foster innovation
- Redefine progress
- Live within means

- Cultivate collaboration
- Ensure equity
- Embrace diversity
- Inspire leadership
- Continuously improve

While each individual and organization can embrace these guiding principles, it will not be enough.

> Large-scale social change requires broad cross-sector coordination,
> yet the social sector remains focused on the isolated intervention
> of individual organizations.
>
> **John Kania and Mark Kramer, "Collective Impact,"** *Stanford Social Innovation Review,*
> **Winter 2011**

Collaboration is nothing new; there are partnerships and joint efforts all around us. However, given what we are currently faced with and will face in the future, **we need a supercharged type of collaboration:** collective impact initiatives. The American Library Association's Center for the Future of Libraries has identified "collective impact" as a prominent trend for libraries to respond to:

> Complex social issues—hunger, poverty, violence, education, health, public safety, the environment—involve many different factors, and responses to these issues include many different community organizations. Organizations working in isolation and/or individual projects have not significantly addressed or changed many of these issues. (www.ala.org/tools/future/trends/collectiveimpact)

In a 2011 article in the *Stanford Social Innovation Review,* John Kania and Mark Kramer defined collective impact as "the commitment of a group of important actors from different sectors to a common agenda for solving a specific social problem" (https://ssir.org/articles/entry/collective_impact). Collective impact is a framework for a structured approach to making collaboration work across sectors: government, business, nonprofit, philanthropic, and individual citizens. The framework calls for each sector to let go of its individual agenda in order to focus on a common agenda.

Kania and Kramer identified five "conditions of collective success":

1. **Common Agenda**—this includes a shared understanding of the problem and a joint approach to solving it through agreed-upon actions.

2. **Shared Measurement Systems**—this condition increases the likelihood for alignment and accountability.

3. **Mutually Reinforcing Activities**—this is a layered plan of action that both outlines and coordinates activities for those agencies and individuals participating in the initiative.

4. **Continuous Communication**—communication is key to building trust, assuring participants that all are being treated fairly and that decisions are made on the basis of objective evidence.

5. **Backbone Support Organizations**—coordination takes time, and it is likely that none of the participating organizations has time to spare. Project management, data management, and facilitation roles must be defined. Adaptive leadership within this support organization must be applied: "the ability to focus people's attention and create a sense of urgency, the skill to apply pressure to stakeholders without overwhelming them, the competence to frame issues in a way that presents opportunities as well as difficulties, and the strength to mediate conflict among stakeholders."

If we take a bird's-eye view of the world around us there is a clear intersection, or sweet spot if you will, that has emerged from the thousands upon thousands of pages of expert analysis, predictions, and proposed solutions: social cohesion. The very nature of disruption is that we do not know what is coming next; we do not know the severity of future disruptions or their exact local impacts. Disruption and disaster, as demonstrated above, can come from many different directions, sometimes all at once. **Our one clear hope is that humanity pulls together to help one another.** Whether that be to prevent disaster, mitigate the impact of disaster, or to recover from disaster, all we have is each other. **We are all in this together.**

RESILIENCE
IN LIBRARIES

IN 2012 I ATTENDED GREENBUILD, THE CONFER-
ence of the U.S. Green Building Council, where I had the
distinct pleasure of hearing a presentation by Alex Wilson,
founder and past president of the well-respected publication
BuildingGreen and president of the Resilient Design Institute
(RDI). RDI defines resilience as "the capacity to adapt to
changing conditions and to maintain or regain **functionality
and vitality** in the face of stress or disturbance. It is the
capacity to bounce back after a disturbance or interruption
of some sort."

I was introduced to *BuildingGreen*, back when it was
Environmental Building News (EBN), when I was pursuing
certification as a sustainable building advisor and accreditation as a Leadership in Energy and Environmental Design
professional (LEED AP). Wilson's work first caught my
eye because, as a librarian, I was impressed that the publication did not accept advertising, which took away much
of the guesswork about whether what I was reading was
"greenwashed."

The other aspect of Wilson's work that caught my eye was his continual advocacy of *passive survivability*—a somewhat unfortunate term that speaks to a very commonsense approach to constructing facilities: building with an eye toward survivability so that in the aftermath of events such as extended power outages, hurricanes, or terrorist attacks, our buildings will be able to provide for our basic needs until power, water, and sewer services are restored. This approach made a lot of sense to me.

I felt that "passive survivability" applied to the way libraries should be thinking about the future of their facilities, for if libraries are essential, as we delight in telling our financial supporters, then we need to take steps to ensure their continued vitality and viability in the face of disaster. As I learned about RDI's design principles, I realized that these apply to more than just the built environment.

In a ballroom packed with architects, engineers, construction managers, and others from the building industry, we got a front-row seat in a master class on how to build for resilience. Lessons learned from the aftermath of Hurricane Katrina were discussed, and Wilson shared the ten Resilient Design Principles that RDI developed in light of these lessons learned:

1. *Resilience transcends scales.* Strategies to address resilience apply at scales of individual buildings, communities, and larger regions and ecosystems; they also apply at different time scales—from immediate to long-term.

2. *Resilient systems provide for basic human needs.* These needs include potable water, sanitation, energy, livable conditions (temperature and humidity), lighting, safe air, occupant health, and food; these should be equitably distributed.

3. *Diverse and redundant systems are inherently more resilient.* More diverse communities, ecosystems, economies, and social systems are better able to respond to interruptions or change, making them inherently more resilient. While sometimes in conflict with efficiency and green building priorities, *redundant* systems for such needs as electricity, water, and transportation improve resilience.

4. *Simple, passive, and flexible systems are more resilient.* Passive or manual-override systems are more resilient than complex solutions that can break down and require ongoing maintenance. Flexible solutions are able to adapt to changing conditions both in the short and long term.

5. *Durability strengthens resilience.* Strategies that increase durability enhance resilience. Durability involves not only building practices, but also building design (beautiful buildings will be maintained and last longer), infrastructure, and ecosystems.

6. *Locally available, renewable, or reclaimed resources are more resilient.* Reliance on abundant local resources, such as solar energy, annually replenished groundwater, and local food provides greater resilience than dependence on nonrenewable resources or resources from far away.

7. *Resilience anticipates interruptions and a dynamic future.* Adaptation to a changing climate with higher temperatures, more intense storms, sea level rise, flooding, droughts, and wildfires is a growing necessity, while non-climate-related natural disasters, such as earthquakes and solar flares, and anthropogenic actions like terrorism and cybercrime also call for resilient design. Responding to change is an opportunity for a wide range of system improvements.

8. *Find and promote resilience in nature.* Natural systems have evolved to achieve resilience; we can enhance our own resilience by relying

on and applying lessons from nature. Strategies that protect the natural environment enhance resilience for all living systems.

9. *Social equity and community contribute to resilience.* Strong, culturally diverse communities in which people know, respect, and care for each other will fare better during times of stress or disturbance. The social aspects of resilience can be as important as physical responses.

10. *Resilience is not absolute.* We must recognize that incremental steps can be taken and that *total resilience* in the face of all situations is not possible. We should implement what is feasible in the short term and work to achieve greater resilience in stages.[22]

As part of the program, Wilson had the audience rank the importance of the ten principles using a mobile app. The results and ensuing conversation are something I will never forget.

The top-ranked principle is one that appears fairly far down the list: number 9.

> *Social equity and community contribute to resilience.* Strong, culturally diverse communities in which people know, respect, and care for each other will fare better during times of stress or disturbance. The social aspects of resilience can be as important as physical responses.

Wilson seemed unsurprised by this result, and he shared research indicating that communities with a tighter social fabric, those in which neighbors are more connected to each other, have a higher survivability rate[23] in the face of natural and man-made disasters than those that are not.

---

22. www.resilientdesign.org/the-resilient-design-principles/.

23. https://talkpoverty.org/2014/08/04/community-climate-change-social-cohesion-can-help-low-income -baltimore-neighborhoods-prepare-disasters/.

UNDERSTANDING, RESPECT, EMPATHY

Let this sink in: in life-threatening situations caused by weather events or humans, communities that are better connected have a higher survivability rate. When you know your neighbors, you have a resource to draw upon to care for one another and find solutions together.

Libraries can play a major role in efforts to increase the resilience of their communities. When we work to increase *understanding, respect, and empathy* among the residents of our community, we are potentially helping to save their lives.

The truth is that this is already at the heart of what we do as libraries—we increase *understanding, respect, and empathy* for others. Through that work, many of life's other challenges can be addressed. **Civil discourse, shared problem-solving, and empathy for our neighbors** are what this world needs more than just about anything else.

In the aftermath of Superstorm Sandy later in 2012, I watched, on the edge of my seat, as libraries in New York responded, not just as sources of information but as boots-on-the-ground support for the neighborhoods they serve. In many cases, librarians were on the ground before the Red Cross arrived. In Queens, librarians were coordinating clothing and food drives, helping people connect with sources for communication, transportation, and other basic needs.[24] Librarians were effective in this setting because of the connections they had established with the patrons

---

24. Ginny Mies, "5 Ways Libraries Support Disaster Relief and Recovery," *TechSoup* (blog), August 25, 2015, http://forums.techsoup.org/cs/community/b/tsblog/archive/2015/08/25/5-ways-libraries-support-disaster-relief-and -recovery.aspx.

they serve—they were a trusted part of the community's support system on a very basic level.

The role of libraries as a **community connector** is vital in the sustainability and resilience of a community.

The IPCC report (*Climate Change 2014: Impacts, Adaptation, and Vulnerability*) mentioned earlier urges *iterative risk management* as a useful framework for decision-making in complex situations, such as the adverse effects of climate change: complex situations are defined as being "characterized by large potential consequences, persistent uncertainties, long timeframes, **potential for learning,** and multiple climatic and non-climatic influences changing over time"[25] (boldface added).

The word *iterative* is key. We need to keep learning, keep trying, keep connecting. It is the only thing that will help us in the end, because **we don't know what is coming next**. Libraries embody the "potential for learning," and have a growing role to play to ensure that people are talking to one another about what they are learning. Moreover, libraries help to preserve open access to data, and they help people analyze what is being learned about the world around us.

Some years ago George Needham, a longtime library consultant, strategist, and library director, coined the phrase *first restorers* to describe the role of libraries in the face of community crisis. We may not be "siren services" or first responders, putting out a fire or wearing riot gear, but we are a significant part of the solution, helping citizens pick up the pieces and find their way forward, or better yet, providing services and programs that help mitigate the risk of disasters happening in the first place.

But we can only be effective as restorers if we've worked continuously to **build trust**—we can't just show up after a problem has occurred.

---

25. www.ipcc.ch/pdf/assessment-report/ar5/wg2/ar5_wgII_spm_en.pdf, p. 9.

This mind-set must be continuous: we are **catalysts and conveners** who continually work to bring people together.

Libraries are perfectly positioned to assist, if not lead, efforts that work to manage risk and build resilience as identified in the IPCC report:

- *Local matters.* Adaptations that will strengthen communities are "place- and context-specific, with no single approach for reducing risks appropriate across all settings."
- *Working together.* "Adaptation planning and implementation can be enhanced through complementary actions across levels, from individuals to governments."
- *Recognize and value diversity.* "Recognition of diverse interests, circumstances, social-cultural contexts, and expectations can benefit decision-making processes."
- *Help all to be heard.* "Increased capacity, voice, and influence of low-income groups and vulnerable communities and their partnerships with local governments also benefit adaptation."

All four of these principles match up beautifully with what libraries are good at already. How fortuitous for us all that *what the world needs most right now is what libraries are already very good at providing*.

- *Local matters.* Libraries are local, to a community, campus, school, or business. A library's promotion of resources to meet local needs, to support local businesses, job-seekers, students, senior citizens, and families is what inspires its stakeholders to continue to invest in the library. Prioritizing local history, recording the oral histories of residents, and preserving memorabilia are what help provide a sense of place with a richness and identity that enable newer and younger residents to connect with longer-term residents. History is part of how we learn to manage the future. Respect for the

"local" and an understanding of what has come before us is part
of resilience planning.

- *Working together.* Libraries can be a hub: of information, learning,
  and conversation. Libraries are natural catalysts and conveners
  to help advance understanding of an issue or to crowd-source
  solutions. A primary role of public libraries, identified in both
  of the major planning models for libraries over the past three
  decades (*Planning and Role Setting for Public Libraries* by McClure,
  and *Strategic Planning for Results* by Nelson), is the library as a
  "community information center." In the latter version, *Strategic
  Planning for Results* by Sandra Nelson, this role is defined as a
  service response in which "residents will have a central source for
  information about the wide variety of programs, services, and
  activities provided by community agencies and organizations." This
  bird's-eye view of the community and who is working on what
  is an invaluable component in mapping a community's human
  resources in order to identify who should be working together on
  larger issues related to the resilience of a community.

- *Recognize and value diversity.* Libraries are for everyone. Libraries
  are one of the few places in our communities where everyone is
  welcome, regardless of their age, background, socioeconomic status,
  or ethnicity. The library is the crossroads of a community where
  people who might otherwise never come together can find common
  ground. This is one of the key ingredients in knitting together a
  tighter social fabric, convening people from diverse backgrounds
  who know and respect one another. In the professional statements
  found below, you can see in the ALA's Library Bill of Rights, "Core
  Values of Librarianship," and "Code of Professional Ethics" the
  emphasis on service *to all,* and on providing access to materials

that represent the widest range of human experiences, not just those of a monoculture. This emphasis on access, exposure, and commitment to diversity is embedded in the very essence of the public library.

- *Help all to be heard.* The library's role as a forum, a nonpartisan platform where people can come together for civil and civic discourse and learn from one another, elevates the understanding, respect, and empathy necessary for social cohesion. Libraries, once again, are perfectly positioned to amplify those who lack a formal "voice" in our community while encouraging and supporting the dialogue that is necessary to come together as a community.

SOCIAL COHESION, EQUITY, ACCESS

In the literature cited earlier in this book, expert after expert came to the conclusion that at the core of a community's resilience is social cohesion.

Social cohesion is defined as a cohesive society that[26]

- Works towards the well-being of its members
- Fights exclusion and marginalization
- Creates a sense of belonging
- Promotes trust
- Offers its members opportunities for upward mobility (rising from a lower to a higher socioeconomic class or status)

Using social cohesion as a **compass setting,** we find that the core values and codes of ethics of libraries are neatly aligned with the goal of helping communities prepare for a resilient future.

---

26. OECD, 2011, "Perspectives on Global Development 2012: Social Cohesion in a Shifting World," OECD Publishing, http://dx.doi.org/10.1787/persp_glob_dev-2012-en.

Let's take a look at the American Library Association's **Library Bill of Rights**:

> The American Library Association affirms that all libraries are forums for information and ideas, and that the following basic policies should guide their services.
>
> I. Books and other library resources should be provided for the interest, information, and enlightenment of **all people of the community** the library serves. Materials should not be excluded because of the origin, background, or views of those contributing to their creation.
>
> II. Libraries should provide materials and information presenting **all points of view** on current and historical issues. Materials should not be proscribed or removed because of partisan or doctrinal disapproval.
>
> III. Libraries should **challenge censorship** in the fulfillment of their responsibility to provide information and enlightenment.
>
> IV. Libraries should cooperate with **all persons and groups** concerned with resisting abridgment of free expression and free access to ideas.
>
> V. A person's right to use a library should not be denied or abridged because of origin, age, background, or views.
>
> VI. Libraries which make exhibit spaces and meeting rooms available to the public they serve should make such facilities available on an **equitable basis**, regardless of the beliefs or affiliations of individuals or groups requesting their use.

Adopted June 19, 1939, by the ALA Council; amended October 14, 1944; June 18, 1948; February 2, 1961; June 27, 1967; January 23, 1980; inclusion of "age" reaffirmed January 23, 1996.

Let's next take a look at the **"Core Values of Librarianship"**:

- Access
- Confidentiality/Privacy
- Democracy
- Diversity
- Education and Lifelong Learning
- Intellectual Freedom
- Preservation
- The Public Good
- Professionalism
- Service
- Social Responsibility

Now check out the ALA's **"Code of Professional Ethics"**:

1. We provide the highest level of service to **all library users** through appropriate and usefully organized resources; equitable service policies; equitable access; and accurate, unbiased, and courteous responses to all requests.
2. We uphold the **principles of intellectual freedom** and **resist all efforts** to censor library resources.
3. We protect **each library user's right to privacy and confidentiality** with respect to information sought or received and resources consulted, borrowed, acquired or transmitted.
4. We respect intellectual property rights and **advocate balance** between the interests of information users and rights holders.
5. We treat co-workers and other colleagues with **respect, fairness, and good faith**, and advocate conditions of employment that **safeguard the rights and welfare** of all employees of our institutions.

6. **We do not advance private interests** at the expense of library users, colleagues, or our employing institutions.

7. **We distinguish between our personal convictions and professional duties** and do not allow our personal beliefs to interfere with fair representation of the aims of our institutions or the provision of access to their information resources.

8. **We strive for excellence** in the profession by maintaining and enhancing our own knowledge and skills, by encouraging the professional development of co-workers, and by fostering the aspirations of potential members of the profession.

All three of these professional statements, the Library Bill of Rights, the "Core Values of Librarianship," and the "Code of Professional Ethics," speak not only to how we have become trusted institutions in today's world, but what the world needs now more than ever: an institution that is focused on **equity and access**.

Equity of **access** is central to these statements—access for all, access to information, access to public gathering spaces, and access to each other. Libraries provide equal access to platforms that can be used to achieve positive change. As noted in the literature, some citizens and communities are more vulnerable than others when confronted with environmental, economic, social, political, and technological disruptions due to socioeconomic factors. These vulnerabilities, which are born out of decades, if not centuries, of decisions made, cannot be reversed overnight. However, these vulnerabilities exist and there is only **one way forward**, and that is together. Applying the core values of libraries is a recipe for our future focus: Access, Confidentiality/Privacy, Democracy, Diversity, Education and Lifelong Learning, Intellectual Freedom, Preservation, the Public Good, Professionalism, Service, and

Social Responsibility. These eleven values provide the building blocks for social cohesion and collective impact.

At the nexus of resilience planning and libraries is the concept of **equity**, the quality of being fair and impartial. The idea is that everyone deserves an equal chance, whether it be for the sake of education or for our very survival. Libraries, if focused on achieving equity, can level the playing field in ways we might never have dreamed possible.

The word "impartial" may be used interchangeably with the word "neutral," and we must acknowledge that the concept of neutrality has been hotly debated in the library profession over the past two years. We must keep in mind that neutrality does not exist in a vacuum. It exists in the context of our profession's core values. If our compass setting is to think sustainably,[27] and we combine our eleven core values with our resources to ensure that our communities thrive, then neutrality is not the absence of ethics; it is the removal of politics from a situation or issue while still adhering to our professional values.

EMPOWER, ENGAGE, ENERGIZE

Libraries encourage citizens to learn to think for themselves, to use information to their best advantage, and to consider the sources of data and information before applying them to decision-making. All of these are critical skills for a resilient society.

Libraries **empower** those they serve to find solutions, to be intellectually curious, and to question the world around them. Libraries **engage** with the patrons they serve in order to understand them, where they are coming from, where they want to go, and then help them get there.

27. Rebekkah Smith Aldrich, *Sustainable Thinking: Ensuring Your Library's Future in an Uncertain World* (Chicago: American Library Association, 2018).

Libraries **energize** their communities, bringing new and energetic life to them through empowerment and engagement. Libraries provide, in the words of David Lankes, a platform for communities to succeed:

> The mission of librarians is to improve society through facilitating knowledge creation in their communities. (David Lankes)[28]

Through our facilities, expert staff, collections, programs, and partnerships, our focus is on enabling the success, the viability, and *the resilience* of those who live in the communities that we serve. These "Three E's of Sustainable Libraries," **Empower, Engage, Energize**, are the keys to resilience planning, for when people are empowered to work together to find solutions that will ensure a better future, there is a necessary, and inspiring, energy that is generated through this type of engagement.

As outlined in my book *Sustainable Thinking: Ensuring Your Library's Future in an Uncertain World,* the Three E's of Sustainable Libraries are a two-way street. A library can empower its patrons to go forth and do good things by engaging with them to understand their hopes and aspirations. And in turn, a community can see and feel the authentic interest a library has in being a part of that community's conversations; the community sees the library at the table, or convening "the table," in efforts to find community-based solutions. When a library engages with its community and shows love and support for the goals and aspirations of those it serves by empowering and energizing patrons through library services, that community turns around and gives empowerment right back to its library in the form of good will and financial investment. This is a sustainable pattern for the future of libraries.

---

28. David R. Lankes, *The Atlas of New Librarianship* (Cambridge, MA: The MIT Press, 2011).

Inside the library:

- *Empower*: All stakeholders—librarians, staff, and the board—are empowered to make the library the best it can be, to find solutions, to own problems, and to step up when necessary.
- *Engage*: All stakeholders feel respected and are included as part of the team that is making the library a success.
- *Energize*: All stakeholders are enthused about the library and where it is going as an organization and, as a result, bring that energy to their work, to the board table, and to community interactions.

With our community:

- *Empower*: Community members are empowered to take control of their lives and the lives of their children and to make their neighborhood a better place through access to information and programs provided by the library.
- *Engage*: Community members think of the library as "theirs" and are engaged with the library board and Friends group or are passionately supportive of the role the library plays in the community.
- *Energize*: Community members feel energized by the library and share that energy to make the library and community better.

A community that is **empowered, engaged, and energized** will envelop the library in the community's lifestyle, consider the library to be a part of the community, and interact with the library in ways that make it part of the neighborhood. Community members own the library, want to see it continue and thrive, and rely on the sustainability of our capacity to serve them.

We, as libraries, do not exist without them, the members of the community. Are we contributing more than just "stuff"? Are we empowering those we come into contact with to truly have a better life? These are the tough questions ahead for library leaders to think through. Much of our profession's current interpretation of our roles is stuck in the old model of libraries, as gatekeepers to information and knowledge. The new model, institutions that are **catalysts and conveners**, is a bold, exciting new role for libraries to step into. We need to leverage our trusted role in our communities to the best advantage in order to further the resilience of those we serve in new and meaningful ways. We need to embrace our role as the "backbone support organizations" that Kania and Kramer noted are critical to the success of collective impact initiatives. Libraries are in a dramatically powerful, influential position to influence the fate of the world.

Libraries have been contributing to social cohesion and community resilience for decades. But there is a sense of urgency emerging as many forward-thinking libraries are stepping up efforts to bring people together, to directly address the challenges that communities face, and to strengthen future-focused choices in order to ensure those communities' maximum viability in the face of disruption. Given the scale and scope of the impact of climate change on our world, nothing less will do.

Abraham Maslow's "hierarchy of needs" is a psychological theory which suggests that people must fulfill basic needs before they can move on to satisfying higher, more advanced needs. The hierarchy is represented as a pyramid with the lower levels, the broad base of the pyramid, made up of the most basic needs—the physical requirements for food, water, sleep, and shelter (figure 2). Once these lower levels have been attained, people are motivated to seek the higher levels.

FIGURE 2

Maslow's Hierarchy of Needs

Part of my day job is helping a number of libraries connect with their communities—to listen to residents' hopes and fears about the future and figure out the role the library will play in the coming years. When I conduct focus groups with library non-users, I try to assess their current perception of libraries in order to help librarians appreciate the fact that what they think they're selling isn't what the outside world is buying.

After close to 250 focus groups, and speaking with more than 2,000 people, my unscientific findings indicate that libraries are often seen— by both outsiders and insiders—as assisting with the upper levels of Maslow's pyramid—self-actualization and self-esteem. However, in times of disruption, when changes in society are wreaking havoc or threatening the basic levels of Maslow's pyramid for a person or a community, the upper levels of the pyramid seem very far away. This aspect seems to me to be key to why we are always on the defensive, trying to prove we are essential: we don't talk about what we do in the context of the lower half of the pyramid.

There is no denying that people without work, who cannot afford to live in the community of their choice, those struggling to find affordable access to healthy food or clean drinking water, those who place a high value on living in a safe place—these people are going to prioritize little else beyond meeting those basic needs. Those who feel unsafe or out of place in their community are unlikely to participate in meaningful ways and feel a sense of love and belonging among their neighbors.

There is the other end of the spectrum as well: middle- and upper-class families and business owners who feel that any shift in social policy may jeopardize their comfort or safety or result in increased taxes. This fear leads to a sense of defensiveness and a "bunker mentality," creating opposition and entrenchment that can result in divisions in a community.

The residents on both sides of this story often feel that the other is the enemy or that the other doesn't understand where they are coming from. This feeling creates tension, adversarial conversations and campaigns, and a general lack of togetherness.

So, what is a library to do?

A growing number of libraries are reassessing their resource deployment in order to address the basic building blocks of the human condition. From libraries that are embedding social workers on staff, to libraries working with neighborhood advocates rather than security personnel to address behavior problems in their library, to libraries stepping up to provide lunch for kids in the summer, I see a shift in attitude toward the issues found at the base of Maslow's pyramid.

——————— ✕ ———————

A post-Maslow theory adds a sixth layer to the pyramid, above self-actualization: **self-transcendence**. Self-transcendence refers to having a higher calling, a higher altruistic goal outside yourself—for your family, neighbors, community, or perhaps the world at large. *This* is where our energy should be focused. Alone we are hopeless, but working together, **we are powerful**. Appealing to people's desire to be useful, to be helpful, to do meaningful work, and to live a better life means we can help support and connect an ever-growing contingent of people who, like us, want to make the world a better place.

Libraries must embody self-transcendence in order to appeal to a broad cross-section of their community. If we ourselves are conveying a bunker mentality by taking a defensive stance through our policies and service design, we become less helpful and less appealing. Only by putting our community at the heart of what we do and how we do it can we "**transcend**" **as libraries**.

We must keep in mind that the disruptions in today's world strike at the very foundation of Maslow's hierarchy of needs. People's lives and livelihoods are at stake, or people are manipulated to feel that this is the case.

Our awareness of and proactive efforts toward minimizing and managing risk in our communities while helping people connect with one another will serve us well in carrying out our educational mission. An unaware library can quickly lose touch with those it serves and diminish the respect and trust that the library would hope to enjoy in its community. We must be mindful of and present with those whom we serve. An attitude of "**we are all in this together**" is the only way forward.

Although it can seem too large a challenge to tackle things like access to food, a healthy environment, poverty, and community safety, these problems will only be attacked by a *systematic* approach that is coordinated across a community, with libraries as part of the strategy.

Many of these challenges are **connected and intertwined**, making for a tough road to finding solutions, but education is a key component to creating a library, neighborhood, and world that are socially equitable, economically feasible, and environmentally sound. Our work is to best position ourselves to **be aware, responsive, and *proactive*** as we design the future of our libraries. Library science can be applied to the issues of the day, but only if we are aware of the issues and understand how they are interconnected with the human experience.

By making bold choices for facility construction, and by stepping out of traditional roles for librarians and taking risks, many leading libraries in our country are not waiting for the government to tell them to do this work. They have a clear vision of the resource allocation decisions necessary to **put their communities at the heart of their libraries**, and to strengthen everything from the built environment to the human condition, all with an eye towards a resilient future.

FROM THE FIELD

IN THE AFTERMATH

When reading about the wider world and resilience and libraries, the lead story is likely to be related to the role libraries play in the aftermath of disruption. From hurricanes to civil unrest, from economic downturns to massive technological shifts, libraries are portrayed as a reactive force, coming to the aid of residents just in time. Libraries are able to play this role thanks to the **trust** they have built up in their neighborhood over time, building on their respected role in the community to help connect their neighbors with the resources and support they need to get through the immediate aftermath of the event and to strengthen themselves for the future.

This role has become so commonplace that in 2010 the U.S. Department of Homeland Security's Federal Emergency Management Agency designated libraries as **essential services**. But innovations in the field have emerged, and libraries are proving that they can be far more than just a spot to plug in or to use the Internet to fill out paperwork.

The **Houston Public Library** (HPL) in Texas had, unfortunately, been through it all before and emerged again as a positive force in the aftermath of 2017's Hurricane Harvey. The lessons learned from Hurricane Ike in 2008, eloquently outlined by HPL director Rhea Brown Lawson and former deputy directors Meller Langford and Roosevelt Weeks in the book *Public Libraries and Resilient Cities*, were quickly and effectively deployed in 2017. HPL staff built on that experience and responded quickly and in some unexpected ways to the hurricane. Harvey left library administrators scrambling to locate and check on their employees and facilities, but they also tried to ensure quick access to what resources they could secure for the good of their community. As reported in *Library Journal:* "Two HPL branches, the McCrain-Kashmere Gardens and McGovern-Stella Link Neighborhood Libraries, were used during the flooding as 'lily pads'—temporary shelter for displaced residents until they can be transported to a more permanent location."[29]

HPL's coordination of services in the hurricane's aftermath helped improve the situation of thousands of residents. Among other efforts, HPL established Recovery Support Centers using their HPL Mobile Express, a "computer lab on wheels," WeCAN community access locations, and computer labs with broadband Internet access located in community centers in high-need neighborhoods. The library also provided a safe and education-based location for child care for municipal employees whose talents were desperately needed in the immediate aftermath of the hurricane. Through these efforts, HPL morphed into the hero that its community needed in its hour of need. However, the

---

29. http://lj.libraryjournal.com/2017/08/public-services/texas-libraries-hit-hard-by-hurricane-harvey/#_.

library's award-winning success in this endeavor would have fallen short had it not *already* been a trusted partner to both those it serves and its municipal partners based on its actions after Hurricane Ike in 2008.

> For at least eight hours a day, while Houston's emergency workers and other essential staff worked to make sure their city recovered from a major crisis, their children were in a well-lit, air conditioned, safe environment, recovering a sense of security and balance in their lives through the structure of the program . . . The 3 R's (relief, recovery, and renewal) became a key tenet embraced by Houston Public Library staff, allowing them to deliver extraordinary service during an extraordinary time.[30]

In the aftermath of Hurricane Harvey, the library directed its archivists to lend their expertise in "preserving and saving precious family memorabilia such as books, letters and photographs that may have been damaged in the storm."[31] When we think of the heart-wrenching losses that so many victims of hurricanes suffer, it can be the small things, such as a photo of a child or parent who is no longer with us, that can bring strength and comfort to a family. In both large and small ways, HPL helped its community cope and recover in humane and thoughtful ways.

New York State of Mind: In New York the 2011–2012 hurricane season was one for the history books. Hurricane Irene in 2011 left much of the Catskill and Hudson Valley regions of upstate New York reeling. Unprecedented flooding from the hurricanes washed away some towns in the mountainous region and caused extended power outages for thousands of residents throughout the Hudson Valley. Libraries became hubs for food and information distribution, and served as gathering

---

30. "In the Wake of Hurricane Ike the Houston Public Library Responds," in *Public Libraries and Resilient Cities*, edited by Michael Dudley, 2013.

31. www.houstonpress.com/news/the-houston-public-library-will-open-doors-at-19-locations-starting-september -5-9757699.

places for the "troops," members of the National Guard deployed to assist with the recovery efforts. It was the simple things that libraries provided which left a lasting impression on residents: a warm meal, a warm smile, and a power strip—the libraries became a place to recharge, both literally and figuratively. From telecommuters left economically stranded in the hurricane's aftermath to a library patron who rolled through the Mahopac Public Library's front doors on the last bit of battery power stored in their life-saving electric wheelchair, libraries sprang into action: power strips, hair dryers, and the suspension of library policies all eased the everyday lives of residents who were scrambling to keep their lives going.

In 2012 a "superstorm," Hurricane Sandy, was one of the worst natural disasters in a generation. In an area quite unprepared for the level of devastation wrought by the storm, library staff from the Far Rockaway branch of the Queens Library in New York City stepped up to the plate. They provided space, expertise, and connections to help residents find their way through an extended period without electricity, heat, food, or Internet connectivity. Library staff, who were themselves without these basic necessities at home, reported for duty to help the neighborhoods they serve on a daily basis, organizing coat drives, a food pantry, and assisting residents to locate the basics of life: water, food, and diapers. The Far Rockaway branch became a hub where donations were dropped off and library employees organized and distributed those donations. The library facility also hosted outpatient medical services provided by visiting nurses whose medical facility had been destroyed by the storm.[32] The library's standing as a trusted, go-to organization connected residents with the building blocks of life in this stressful chapter of the neighborhood's history. The photos of this story that

32. https://americanlibrariesmagazine.org/2012/12/28/the-library-as-lifeline-getting-past-superstorm-sandy/.

stand out the most are those of young children, wrapped in warm clothing, munching on a snack while sitting on mattresses, on what looks like a beach, while library staff read to them. In the background adults are hustling, carrying armfuls of coats and bags of canned goods, and suddenly you realize that the "beach" is actually a parking lot. So much sand was displaced by the storm that a parking lot looked like a beach. Yet in the aftermath these young children are safe, warm, and cared for thanks to a community that pulled together with the help of intrepid library staff whose calling went beyond being information professionals to that of good neighbors.

The **Ferguson Municipal Library** in Missouri came into the national spotlight in 2014 when their response to civil unrest became a new hallmark of libraries recognized for contributing to the resilience of their communities. The Ferguson Municipal Library in Missouri stayed open as schools and other services in their city closed down in the face of civil unrest following the news that a grand jury would not indict police officer Darren Wilson in the killing of Michael Brown, a young African American man.

> Because of the Grand Jury decision, many organizations will be closed, but the Ferguson Municipal Public Library will stay open as long as it is safe for patrons and staff. If the Ferguson-Florissant schools close, we will be hosting activities for the children. We will do everything in our power to serve our community. Stay strong and love each other. (Ferguson Library Twitter Account, 11.24.2014)

This library's simple act of staying open and talking about why they were staying open demonstrated the love, care, and strength that this community so desperately needed. In the face of what many felt was the disintegration of the social fabric in their community, the library gave people hope. The library became a beacon of light in the darkness of those days, and it helped those who wanted to make things better come together to learn from one another and lean on one another. Inside the library, teachers set up shop for kids and parents who were ready to learn despite the school district's postponement of the school year in light of the uncertainty surrounding the civil unrest; they called their pop-up program at the library "School for Peace." Kids were given "healing kits"—backpacks stuffed with books, worksheets, and teddy bears. Leaders are often people who articulate what we are feeling better than we can, and this library eloquently articulated what many people in this community were feeling—that community means family and family sticks together. We are here for one another when tough things happen, and we learn together. Ferguson's library director, Scott Bonner, continuously stressed in interviews with the national media that what he did was "not notable, just noticeable."[33] In an interview with *Buzz-Feed*, he explained that "this is totally, exactly, right in the wheel house of what any library does, what every library does. We have a dramatic moment, and a dramatic circumstance caught the nation's attention, but this is exactly what libraries do every day."[34]

IN THE PLANNING

Lessons learned from past disasters and preparation for what is coming next are heralding exciting developments in new library construction and renovation projects. In looking to get ahead of predicted shortfalls of natural resources and disruptions of the supply of resources due to

33. R. Miller, "It's What We Do: Service and Sanctuary in Ferguson," *Library Journal*, September 15, 2014, http://lj.libraryjournal.com/2014/09/opinion/editorial/its-what-we-do-service-and-sanctuary-in-ferguson-editorial/.
34. M. Zeman, "The Little Library That Lent a Hand: Ferguson Municipal Public Library," *Public Libraries Online*, February 12, 2015, http://publiclibrariesonline.org/2015/02/the-little-library-that-lent-a-hand-ferguson-municipal-public-library/.

the effects of climate change—from flooding to extended power outages and food scarcity—libraries are exploring thoughtful and groundbreaking solutions in the design and construction of their buildings across the county.

While twenty years ago it was only the rare library that used sustainable design strategies to create healthier, smarter facilities, the widespread adoption of the Leadership in Energy and Environmental Design (LEED) standard in the construction industry has resulted in a sharp rise in the number of new library facilities constructed using the LEED standard as their guide to building high-performing facilities with a great financial return on investment.

In a clear move that serves as a watershed moment in the history of library facilities, *Library Journal*'s New Landmark Libraries program requires entries to demonstrate excellence in sustainability. While there is still work to be done to institutionalize sustainable design as a prerequisite for public library facilities, we've made great strides and more often than not, sustainable design is playing a prominent role in both celebrated facilities and more modest, rural facilities. The King County Library System in Washington was named a 2016 Innovator by the Urban Libraries Council for their adoption of LEED standards:

> Exercising prudent fiscal management of taxpayer dollars is critical for public agencies. With soaring energy prices and stricter environmental regulations, employing eco-friendly building strategies helps control operating costs by managing resources efficiently. Equally important is recognizing the effects that building components have on human health and the environment. KCLS is committed to utilizing sustainable design principles that reduce negative impacts on the environment—without sacrificing employee

or patron comfort—and allow taxpayers to realize a strong return
on investment in their communities.[35]

Why does this matter? Sustainable design helps a library make better
choices as an employer, community partner, and global citizen when
it comes to some very basic elements of a resilient world. From the air
we breathe to the resources we consume in constructing and operating
buildings, sustainable design certification programs, like LEED, Green
Globes, and the Living Building Challenge, provide the framework necessary to make better choices and measure the results of those choices.
Libraries not incorporating such standards into their building programs
will increasingly be viewed as out of touch and as poor stewards of the
public's trust. These are institutions that are more concerned with the
bottom line than with the triple bottom line which balances economic
feasibility with environmental stewardship and social equity.

A major global concern is energy conservation. In the United States,
buildings account for 40 percent of carbon dioxide emissions and they
consume 70 percent of the electricity load.[36] The fossil fuel-based energy
economy is shifting, and municipalities and architects are working hard
to transform the built environment from a major contributor of greenhouse gas emissions to a central part of the solution to the climate crisis.

The International Panel on Climate Change's *Fifth Assessment
Report* confirms the need for immediate and sustained action on climate change, detailing how dire the situation is for humanity. The
underlying conclusion of the report is that the time has arrived for
taking the necessary steps to **preserve livable conditions on earth.** A
central way to do this is to minimize the burning of fossil fuels, aiming

---

35. "Building Green: A Healthy and Sustainable Approach," 2016 Innovations, Health, Safety and Sustainability,
https://www.urbanlibraries.org/building-green—a-healthy-and-sustainable-approach-innovation-1299.php?page_id=534.
36. U.S. Energy Information Administration, 2012.

for a complete phase-out by 2050.[37] **One key way to do this is to reduce and ultimately phase out the carbon dioxide emissions of the building sector by transforming the way buildings are designed, built, and operated.**

The **Phoenicia Library** in New York is slated to be the first public library in the United States to be certified under the Passive House Institute US (PHIUS). Buildings designed and built to the PHIUS+ 2015 Passive Building Standard consume 86 percent less energy for heating and 46 percent less energy for cooling when compared to code-compliant buildings.[38] They achieve this through construction techniques, product choices (such as windows and doors), and the engineering of their mechanical systems. The **John Trigg Ester Library** in Alaska is likely to be the second certified Passive House library facility in the United States. They are going further in their design than Phoenicia, with a goal to create a net-zero energy (ZE) facility. [39]

Two bold libraries have already taken their place in history by becoming the first ZE library buildings in the country. These buildings produce as much energy as they use over the course of a year on site. ZE uses exemplary building design, often called "passive design," to minimize energy requirements, and combines this with renewable energy systems that meet these reduced energy needs.[40]

The first ZE library facility in the country was a 2,400-square-foot branch of the **Lincoln Heritage Public Library** system in Chrisney, Indiana, built in 2009.[41] The next was the **West Branch library** in Berkeley, California, the first certified Living Building Challenge ZE public library in the state. The West Branch library, built in 2013 and named

37. https://www.ipcc.ch/pdf/assessment-report/ar5/wg3/ipcc_wg3_ar5_summary-for-policymakers.pdf.
38. www.phius.org/home-page.
39. https://www.esterlibrary.org/wp-content/uploads/2011/12/TPS63265short.pdf.
40. https://www.wbdg.org/resources/net-zero-energy-buildings.
41. https://living-future.org/lbc/case-studies/chrisney-branch-library-lincoln-heritage-public-building/.

one of the American Institute of Architects' 2016 Top Ten Projects, is a 9,500-square-foot facility. Zero energy buildings, as certified by the Living Future Institute, have "best in class" energy-efficient improvements of 60–90 percent over the baseline[42] and do not use fossil fuels.

One to watch: In the works is the **Hayward Public Library's** 21st Century Library and Heritage Plaza project. This library is projected not just to be the largest ZE public library in the United States, but the largest ZE *building* in the country. It will be completely powered by renewable solar energy and will generate surplus clean energy.[43]

IN THE COMMUNITY

As discussed earlier in this book, critical to a resilient society is social cohesion; this entails communities in which people know one another and respect, empathize, and understand one another. Libraries further this routinely through traditional educational programs for children, young adults, and, increasingly, adults of all ages. From celebrations of Martin Luther King Jr. Day to National Hispanic Heritage Month and hyper-local cultural events that represent local enclaves of diversity, libraries have been working to incorporate programs that connect neighbors with neighbors across ethnic and social divides.

Innovators in this area:

The **Topeka & Shawnee County Public Library** in Kansas, the 2016 Gale/Library Journal Library of the year, has gone beyond the traditional role of providing programming to that of a convener of conversations. Encouraging two-way communication, the library trains staff, members of nonprofit groups, and general community volunteers as "community

---

42. https://living-future.org/net-zero/.
43. www.haywardlibrary.org/post/92885994134/what-is-net-zero-energy.

facilitators," individuals able to convene meetings with a skill set that includes "listening without judging, maintaining confidentiality, finding and synthesizing information, and valuing diverse perspectives." To date the library has forty-two trained facilitators who run meetings both inside and outside of the library. "Conversations focus on topics such as increasing collective health, battling poverty and homelessness, creating work-readiness programs, growing broadband access, feeding children, and supporting young professionals. At these talks, the library offers resources and identifies needs it can fulfill."[44]

The **Madison Public Library's** Library Takeover: Make [Your Idea Here] Happen at Your Library. After making a concerted effort to hear from segments of the community that were least represented in public libraries through a decentralized "Tell Us" in-person survey campaign, the Madison (Wisconsin) Public Library (MPL) partnered with the Madison Public Library Foundation to create a community-driven framework for developing adult programming. Library Takeover invited applications from teams of three to five community members, who were not affiliated with a nonprofit or institution, to create their own large-scale events using the library as the platform. The initial Takeover program received thirty-nine applications! Three teams were chosen, and the program provided a six-week event-planning boot camp with local experts to help team members plan their events. The events produced included a dance party preceded by a discussion on the ways that night-life spaces can be inaccessible to members of the community; a gathering of local poets, writers, spoken-word performers, hip-hop artists, and storytellers that brought the Madison writing community together; and a celebration of local Indian-American culture that attracted more

44. http://lj.libraryjournal.com/2016/06/awards/2016-galelj-library-of-the-year-topeka-shawnee-county-public-library
-ks-leveraging-leadership/#_.

than 400 people. "It's about publicly and loudly committing library resources—whatever those may be—so that community members have an opportunity to host their own events," said Laura Damon-Moore, the community engagement librarian at MPL, at a discussion session at the ALA's Annual Conference in 2017.

The **Howard County Library System's** "Choose Civility" community-wide initiative resulted in an attention-grabbing program in 2017, "The Longest Table." The initiative's mission values diversity and emphasizes respect, compassion, empathy, and inclusiveness as essential to quality of life. The event, the first of its kind in Maryland, brought together a diverse group of more than 300 guests to share a meal (at a *very* long table!) and engage in meaningful conversation about their community. The event provided a setting for guests to share their experiences, gain an understanding of how to find common ground, and move their community forward together.[45] Choose Civility programming continues on through the library system with programs related to information literacy, the importance of having difficult conversations around race and patriotism, good sportsmanship, and kindness. The initiative issues a monthly "Random Acts of Civility Calendar" that helps residents to be positive and focus their energy on activities that support the community. The list of partners and sponsors of the initiative is truly impressive. "Valuing diversity, we choose respect, compassion, empathy, and inclusiveness as essential to our quality of life." Learn more here: http://choosecivility.org/.

One to watch: the **School of Information Studies (iSchool) at Syracuse University** in New York has received a National Leadership Grant from the Institute of Museum and Library Services to create a workflow for libraries to assess community learning needs; identify community experts' interests and availability to offer their expertise; and build data

---

45. http://choosecivility.org/.

models to capture needs and people resources as a "collection" of human resources based at the libraries. This idea extends the popular "human library" or "human book" program idea, in which program attendees get to "check a neighbor out of the library" to have a conversation, and it creates a lasting community database of expertise that is surfaced and readily accessible. The goal of the project is to develop a workflow process for librarians to catalog, coordinate, and promote this collective human expertise. This program celebrates the wisdom of local experts and helps connect neighbors with neighbors, perfectly exemplifying the idea that to be resilient we need to know one another and work together.

IN THE PREPARATION

One of the most exciting, and underestimated, trends in libraries is the concentrated efforts to promote self-sufficiency in the natural and future world—empowering citizens to "**hack the world**." While we may not know what disruptions lie ahead in our personal future or the future of our community, one thing we do know is that we will need people who understand how the world works and how to "hack" it to find solutions to shared problems. Libraries that are creating an environment which encourages and nurtures the creative and curious spirit, and that are excited by people who want to learn how to do things, are generating an engaged generation who can navigate this world, come what may.

When 3-D printers first came on the scene and the Fayetteville Free Library in New York kick-started the makerspace craze in libraries, many old-school library leaders were dismissive, thinking this was just the latest trend in technology that would fade out in a few years, and that it was certainly not something around which to redesign library spaces and staffing patterns.

But what many in the field were missing was the regenerative nature of makerspaces, the empowerment provided through tinker shops, repair cafés, and hackathons to those in our community seeking to make their world a better place. These services and programs, which are often brought to life with partnerships in the technology sector of our business and higher education communities, are not solely about technology but about teaching people *how to hack the world.*

In hacking parlance, there are "black hat hackers" and "white hat hackers." Black hat hackers are those we fear, perpetrators of the coding mayhem that enables criminal acts such as holding your data for ransom or releasing sensitive and personal information, invading your privacy.

White hat hackers use their coding prowess for good, to create solutions to societal problems through technology. For example, Urb.ag, a web app from Fathom Information Design, helps the residents of Boston figure out how to start an urban farm in their city. The app walks a potential farmer through the process of submitting applications, obtaining permits, and even attending public hearings if necessary, with all the information tailored to the exact code that applies to the would-be farm's address. This technology empowers residents with data to do something that is so basic—grow their own food, which is a particularly critical issue in urban environments. Civic hackathons across the country are inspiring programmers to access open data sets provided by the government in order to improve decision-making and identify opportunities. In Los Angeles, the Hack for L.A. event resulted in twenty-two solutions to civic issues, including the winning app of the event, Pool Party. Pool Party encourages people attending the same get-togethers to carpool, walk, bike, or take public transportation in groups in order to reduce their ecological footprint and help maintain active lifestyles. When a user enters their destination, the app shows all available modes of transportation and identifies others nearby who are going to the event.[46]

When we think about teaching people to code, the conversation is usually centered on workforce development, but we should also be weaving in awareness of how to *hack the world for good* through this skill set.

Libraries that offer repair cafés, like the Boulder (CO) Public Library's U-Fix-It Clinic, are doing something quite similar. The extension of traditional library services to include not only lectures or discussion-style programming, but also hands-on experiential learning opportunities, empowers people to learn about the world around them and take control of the multitude of "things" in their life. An increasing number of items in our households—from our toasters to our computers—are designed to fail; they are designed to have an end of useful life in order to compel you to buy the next new thing. This built-in obsolescence is an economic, environmental, and therefore a societal problem that adds to the toxicity and volume of our landfills and means more cash out of our pockets. Teaching people how things work and how to repair them while providing space to share skills and tools can lead to innovative solutions that extend the useful life of an item or recreate or invent the next new thing.

Part of being sustainable is lowering our level of consumption ("**Reduce**, Reuse, Recycle"); part of being resilient is fixing our own stuff when it breaks; and part of being (re)generative can be inventing our own solution to meet our needs. These types of services in libraries speak to the pioneering spirit that we would hope to instill in our young people so that they have the skills to make the world better, on their own terms.

---

46. https://technical.ly/2015/06/09/6-awesome-projects-years-national-day-civic-hacking/.

Innovators in this area:

The **Desmond Fish Library** in Garrison, New York, is home to one of the earliest coding programs for kids in a public library in the United States: Project Code Spring (PCS). Kids learn to code, build their own laptops and robots, and interact with cutting-edge technology. The stated goals of PCS are "to create a framework of best practices for communities to support technological literacy, foster creativity and innovation, and instill a lifelong passion for tinkering, creating and hacking. We want to make it easy for parents, teachers and interested tech-savvy citizens to make experiences for kids that put them on a path of discovery, enjoyment and imagination around technology." The library's dedicated space for this program includes an augmented reality sandbox which combines a data projector and sensor that are used in a fun and interactive way to learn about geography, water flow, erosion, and so on, which are all important environmental factors in their region. The augmented reality landscape responds in real time to the kids playing in the sand; for instance, they can create a shadow over the landscape with their hands that would result in rainfall on the area below. They can dig in the sand and create valleys and gorges for water to flow through. The library has loaned the setup to the school's science department so they can integrate it into their environmental science curriculum, to talk about things like watersheds and how chemical runoff can affect the water supply. Inspired by the overwhelming community demand for access to Project Code Sprint and associated programs, the library has just significantly upgraded their space to include the Innovation & Learning Center, which boasts various technology applications to support creative and collaborative projects.

The **Princeton Public Library** in New Jersey is an active collaborator in Code for Princeton, "a group of techies and community members interested in open government and civic hacking." The group hosts "hack nights," workshops, and talks, and it works with the municipal government to provide open data sets. The group held their first "hackathon" in 2015 and teams worked on a variety of projects, including a website to track the city's gas and electricity usage and provide information on the impact of energy use by Princeton residents on greenhouse gas emissions. At one of their hack night events, coders worked to create a bicycle crash map in their downtown area for the past twelve years thanks to a data set provided by the police department. As a result, the maps were used by the Princeton Complete Streets Committee to make recommendations to the Planning Board for the Bicycle Master Plan. The team built a website, Bike View (www.bikeview.org/en/), where people can see the crash maps and report bicycle-related incidents or road conditions which are forwarded to Access Princeton, the town's app for resident feedback.

The **Pikes Peak Library District** in Colorado has been a pioneer in reconnecting residents with skills that have been lost in our society over the past few generations, from gardening, beekeeping, and canning to raising chickens and xeriscaping; these old-school survival skills (sometimes called "homesteading" skills) help reconnect residents with their food supply and the land around their homes. The library devotes an entire "Green Team" Facebook Page to the promotion of sustainability and building awareness of responsible environmental stewardship in and beyond the Pikes Peak Library District.

The library district's programs and classes promote self-sufficiency, which is an important skill set when thinking about resilience. Should food supply chains be disrupted due to a natural disaster, terrorism, or some other, perhaps currently inconceivable reason, people who know how to grow, prepare, and preserve their own food will be very valuable.

Homesteading skills can include not only agricultural topics like growing your own food, but also a focus on repurposing and recycling, home remedies, homemade cleaning products, sewing, composting, foraging, first aid, bike repair, and basic car repair—all things that encourage self-resilience and instill a do-it-yourself mentality that is key to problem-solving.

COLLECTIVE IMPACT

The **Rochester Public Library (RPL)** in New York is a member of the Rochester-Monroe Anti-Poverty Initiative (RMAPI), a collaborative community initiative to overcome poverty in the City of Rochester and in Monroe County. In 2015 the City of Rochester was ranked first on a list of similarly sized cities for "extreme poverty." This means the city has more people *living at less than half* the federal poverty level than any other similarly sized city in the United States.[47] It is the only city of its size where slightly more than half of the children live in poverty. RMAPI's vision is that every child and family will have the opportunity to live in a stable environment where the promise of economic mobility is a reality. Their goal is to reduce poverty in the region by 15 percent in 5 years, 30 percent in 10 years, and 50 percent over the next 15 years. RMAPI has involved the efforts and input of nearly 1,000 people in the region, including more than 200 volunteers on committees and work groups. Importantly, there is significant emphasis placed on the participation of individuals who are personally impacted by poverty. The work done by this group is an excellent example of a "collective impact initiative." Many activities will be necessary to address the themes the group has identified: the need for community-building, and efforts to overcome

---

47. www.democratandchronicle.com/story/news/2015/01/08/rochester-poverty-act-community-foundation-report/21452093/.

structural racism and alleviate poverty-induced trauma. An example of how the city is banding together to figure this out can be found in the poverty simulations held to help increase understanding and empathy around the issue. Poverty simulations help community leaders, health and human service providers, area businesses, and other community stakeholders "deepen their understanding of the day-to-day challenges faced by those living in poverty and how current systems, policies, and practices create barriers."[48] Increasing respect, understanding, and empathy among stakeholders who have the power and license to make things better is an activity that can empower the leaders of the city to think differently, more sustainably, about the future.

The library has had one of the most visible wins in this effort so far; it was awarded the 2017 Joseph F. Shubert Library Excellence Award for its pilot program to eliminate library fines.

> The library, in its efforts to address the endemic problem of poverty in its community, identified and documented usage trends and existing financial barriers to using the library. With clear goals to increase access and circulation of library materials among families living in poverty, the RPL gained approval from its Trustees and incorporated anticipated adjustments into the City's annual budget before proceeding with its bold program. The RPL pilot ran from July 1, 2016 to June 30, 2017. During this period, children's and young adult materials owned by the RPL did not accrue daily overdue fines. The pilot, which saw a 10% increase in circulation of materials over the previous year, was well received by the community and was praised by the Mayor of Rochester, who announced that the fines elimination on materials for children and teens would be made permanent. Most importantly, the program had positive

---

48. https://www.ccsi.org/Programs/Poverty-Simulation.

benefits on children and families and erased a disincentive to using the library for residents living in poverty.[49]

"I haven't worked with a more powerful concept than collective impact in my entire career," said Patricia Uttaro, long-time director of the Monroe County Library System, which includes RPL. "It is hard work getting people and organizations to let go of the 'me/mine first, me/mine only' attitude, and it's not always successful. When it *is* successful, the results are definitely worth the challenge." The Rochester Public Library is leading by example, walking the walk of an ethical library truly putting the aspirations of its residents above long-standing policies that have created inequities for the young people of their city.

A growing number of libraries are using the American Library Association's **Libraries Transforming Communities** resources[50] to "turn outwards" and identify shared community goals and surface partners that should be working together on collective impact initiatives. These libraries are taking the initiative to put their communities at the heart of the library by seeking widespread input to answer four vital questions:

1. What kind of community do you want to live in?
2. Why is that important to you?
3. How is that different from how you see things now?
4. What are some of the things that need to happen to create that kind of change?

These libraries, servicing communities large and small, become catalysts for change just by asking these questions. Some of the libraries have gone on to convene groups and conversations that begin the collaborative

---

49. www.nysl.nysed.gov/libdev/adviscns/rac/award/index.html.
50. www.ala.org/tools/librariestransform/libraries-transforming-communities/turning-outward.

work that is necessary to address large problems faced by communities. You can read the stories of early adopter libraries at www.ala.org/tools/librariestransform/libraries-transforming-communities/turning-outward.

The outcomes are notable not only for the particular library service and program decisions made by these libraries, but for the fact that these libraries are the spark that brings community members and agencies together to find solutions to common problems.

The **library as catalyst** is the calling card of the modern library.

FOR THE FUTURE

... the future already has begun.

Alvin Toffler, *Future Shock*

THE HARD TRUTH ABOUT THE FUTURE IS THAT libraries are behind the curve on many of the issues that other institutions and industries have raced ahead on. There are examples here and there but few are systemically focused institution-wide. While we are **perfectly positioned** to have a larger positive impact, *we need to work faster and deeper*.

The signs are clear, and the data doesn't lie: we should all feel an **urgency** around our participation in preparing for a more resilient future. The future mission of libraries, should we choose to accept it, may not sound that much different than what we have done for decades: to participate in the co-creation of a resilient society that can endure shocks and rebuild itself when necessary, and hopefully emerge stronger and better than before. However, the urgency surrounding us, *given the severity of what lies ahead,* particularly on the environmental front, means that libraries need to **deliberately** hone their capacity to anticipate, plan, and adapt for the future—and help those they serve do the same—at a much faster, stronger, and deeper pace.

Now is the time to be focused, deliberate, and clear about our goals. Every aspect of library operations, services, programs, and outreach—can contribute to a more resilient society.

Libraries, as established earlier, are one of the best-positioned institutions in the country to assist in co-creating a resilient society. They are

- Dedicated to the preservation of access to information and ideas
- Committed to intellectual freedom
- Focused on creating an informed citizenry in the name of democracy
- Situated in every county, city, town, and village in the country

Libraries are **connectors, conveners, and catalysts** that bring ideas and people together to improve life, liberty, and the pursuit of happiness. The work now is to hone these skills and attributes with urgency, because lives depend on our efforts.

OPPORTUNITIES FOR THE FUTURE

"Is time long, or is it wide?" I found this quote by artist Laurie Anderson in *The Clock of the Long Now: Time and Responsibility* by Stewart Brand, who is best known as the editor of *Whole Earth Catalog*.

> Is time long, or is it wide?
>
> **Laurie Anderson, artist**

Brand interprets Anderson's question:

> [T]ime can be thought of in terms of everything-happening-now-and-last-week-and-next-week (wide) or as a deep-flowing process in which centuries are minor events (long). The wide view sees events as most influenced by what is happening at the moment. The long view perceives events as most influenced by history: "Much was decided before you were born." The wide view is disparaged as short-term thinking. The long view is praised as responsible.

We need to leverage the wide view in order to improve the long view.

Starting *now,* we need to get our act together and move forward with conviction and purpose. What we do now can lay the foundation for a solid future for libraries if we are working on the right things, sending the right messages, building the right partnerships, and making a difference that matters.

Value Set

Libraries would be well served to **adopt sustainability as a core value**; in fact, the entire profession would be well served by doing so. What if, like the West Vancouver Memorial Library, we adopt the core value of sustainability for our institutions? The West Vancouver (British Columbia) Memorial Library first formally adopted sustainability as a core value in its 2010–2015 Strategic Plan:

> **Sustainability**: We manage our resources responsibly to enhance our financial stability, social goodwill, and environmental leadership.

Then the library evolved. In its 2016–2020 Strategic Plan, the library once again adopted sustainability as a core value but turned the phrase outward:

Sustainability: We manage our resources responsibly to maintain financial, social, and environmental sustainability for the well-being of our community.

The West Vancouver Memorial Library went from being focused on the library's sustainability to being focused on the community's sustainability. This outlook is at the heart of sustainable thinking for libraries. If we manage and deploy our resources—from our staff and facilities to our services and programs—with an eye toward sustainability, we strengthen not only ourselves but our communities.

This compass setting should set the stage for the changes, adjustments, and future organizational planning that will be necessary for libraries to inspire the changes, advances, and adaptations that will be necessary in the wider world.

Adopting a core value of sustainability is a message that will inspire people from all walks of life to invest in our institutions and listen to us when engaged in resilience planning in their communities. But one harsh truth is an obstacle in our efforts to contribute to the development of a more resilient society: many people outside the library profession (and, unfortunately, some still in the profession) have lost sight of why libraries do what they do. Most people barely know *what* we do, let alone why and how we do these things. This hinders our access to wider community conversations, government planning, and funding streams that are related to resilience planning. We need to get better at talking about *why* we do what we do and why we are a natural partner in resilience planning, or a decline in investment is exactly what will happen.

We can start by visibly adopting a commitment to the well-being of our communities rather than simply assuming that community leaders understand why we do what we do; this would be a strong start to clearing the path for libraries to have a seat at the table.

The following readiness recommendations are broken into four categories:

- Acute: Inside Your Library
- Acute: In Your Community
- Long-Term: Inside Your Library
- Long-Term: In Your Community

There is an urgency around resilience planning which can make many libraries feel a sense of panic or dread, and which can lead to paralysis or a shotgun approach to planning. However, what is called for is a **systematic** approach to working through risk assessment and response measures. In the remaining sections of this chapter, recommendations are broken into two basic categories: "Acute Readiness" recommendations refer to basic things that a library should have on its radar to prepare for the future. "Acute" refers to mitigation strategies for bad, difficult, or unwelcome situations or phenomena that are short in duration but are typically severe situations. "Long-Term Readiness" recommendations refer to long-haul thinking strategies and tactics that, if addressed now, will better position a community for a resilient future.

ACUTE READINESS: INSIDE YOUR LIBRARY

How ready is your library for an acute event that could disrupt the lives of those you serve and your staff? Depending on where you live, you may be faced with the possibility of hurricanes, flooding, wildfires, earthquakes, or other severe environmental events that happen quickly. Moreover, all communities have a risk for civil unrest, mass shootings, or terrorist attacks. These potentially dangerous situations can arise in an instant and libraries, as essential community service points, need to be ready. It is time to **get serious about disaster preparedness and business continuity planning.**

The New Jersey State Library has taken a leading role in helping libraries across the country address disaster preparedness and own their role in community resilience. Their publication, "The Librarian's Disaster Planning and Community Resilience Guidebook" and accompanying workbook are designed to help library leaders "to be better prepared to accept the new mantle of responsibility being thrust on them as a safe haven in times of crises." The Guidebook contains a Four-Step Risk Assessment that helps library leaders identify those risks that are likely to threaten your library.[51]

The NJSL resources will help you get the context you need to prepare and think through the various scenarios that could impact your community. Next, consider the **American Red Cross Ready Rating Program**. All Ready Rating program steps and recommendations are grounded in scientific research, best practices, and expert opinion from respected professionals representing multiple disciplines and perspectives.[52] The program systematically assists an organization with:

- **Emergency Planning**
  - Knowing your region and the types of disasters most likely to impact your business
  - Obtaining a Hazard Vulnerability Assessment from your local emergency management agency
  - Considering which hazards your facility is most likely to experience, based on proximity and past events

---

51. https://www.njstatelib.org/services_for_libraries/resources/disaster_planning/.
52. https://www.readyrating.org/How-It-Works/Essential-Steps-to-Preparedness.

- Knowing your library's current capacity to prepare for, respond to, and recover from a disaster
- Assessing the physical capacity, supplies, equipment, and human resources of your facility to resist damage during a disaster

- **Develop an Emergency Action Plan**
  - Forming an emergency planning committee that is responsible for developing and implementing an emergency response plan
  - Developing a written plan describing how your library will respond during a disaster or medical emergency. Ready Rating members have access to an EAP template generator which will assist you in developing an OSHA-compliant EAP.
  - Creating a Continuity of Operations Plan (COOP)

- **Implement your EAP**
  - Training employees on a regular basis about what to do during a disaster or emergency
  - Acquiring and maintaining needed safety equipment and emergency preparedness supplies
  - Showing employees how to be prepared at work and at home so they are better equipped to help the library respond to and recover from an emergency
  - Conducting and assessing regular drills and exercises to determine the readiness of your employees and facilities

- **Help your community get prepared**
  - Hosting blood drives
  - Contributing supplies and/or services to emergency response efforts

– Working with other agencies to support their disaster and emergency preparedness programs[53]

The past few years have highlighted the harsh realities of civil unrest in our communities. Civil unrest, also referred to as "civil disorder," means "any public disturbance involving acts of violence by assemblages of three or more persons, which cause an immediate danger of or results in damage or injury to the property or person of any other individual."[54] A new form of preparedness planning you may not have encountered before 2017 is "**discordant action emergency**" **planning**. How will your library respond in the face of civil unrest, or predicted civil unrest, in your community? How can you best provide essential services while balancing safety issues? Traditional emergency preparedness training and resources are evolving to consider the implications of civil unrest on organizations; however, libraries may have **a distinct and critical role** to play that is different than the average business or social service agency. Our professional commitment to freedom of speech and expression calls upon us to carefully consider the messages we send, **both verbal and nonverbal**, in the face of such unrest. We should learn from the experiences of those libraries that have already borne the weight of decision-making when faced with these types of events: Ferguson, Baltimore, Charlottesville. There are decisions to be made before, during, and after these events. Libraries that think through their choices and responses ahead of time will be better prepared to have a positive impact on their community and help strengthen and protect that community from future civil unrest.

It is impossible to prepare for every eventuality; therefore, libraries will need to **incubate an innovative spirit among staff**. But creating a

---

53. Adapted from American Red Cross Ready Rating™, "Essential Steps to Preparedness," https://www.ready rating.org/How-It-Works/Essential-Steps-to-Preparedness.
54. https://www.law.cornell.edu/uscode/text/18/232.

"department of innovation" or "innovation coordinator" (even if that is just the director) merely isolates the idea of innovation in your organization. Instead, we need to find ways to encourage, empower, and energize staff around **distributed or open-source innovation** so that staff, and even patrons, are invited to make things better. This practice will serve you well when the floodwaters come.

Taking the **sharing economy** to new levels: many libraries across the country are cultivating nontraditional collections, such as lending gardening tools, drones, sewing machines, and camping equipment. Some have even created new types of libraries within their library, like seed libraries. We need this to become commonplace. Positioning libraries as the **facilitators** of the local sharing economy puts us squarely on the radar of sustainable and resilience thinking in our communities. Can libraries be thinking even bigger? How about an array of solar solutions like solar chargers for handheld devices or portable solar panels that could be deployed in the event of an extended power outage or at outdoor community events?

ACUTE READINESS: IN YOUR COMMUNITY

Libraries can provide the perfect platform to educate community members about preparedness for acute events. We have meeting spaces, a reputation for quality programming in the community, and we appeal to residents of all ages and are a trusted institution. Occasional programming and outreach related to disaster preparedness is evident in libraries today, but libraries are hardly known for participating in community readiness. There is a role for libraries to step into to **be more visible and consistently involved**. Libraries should learn about resilience planning efforts in their community: Who are the players? Is a resilience or disaster preparedness plan already in place? Is there a **Community Emergency Response Team** the library could join? If there is infrastructure already in place, get involved. Be a dedicated member of these efforts. If you discover that your community does not have such an effort or team in place, the library can spearhead getting such efforts off the ground. The U.S. Department of Homeland Security's **Citizen Corps program** provides the resources and structure to do just that.

The mission of the Citizen Corps program is to "harness the power of every individual through education, training, and volunteer service to make communities safer, stronger, and better prepared to respond to the threats of terrorism, crime, public health issues, and disasters of all kinds through:

- Preparing the public for local risks with targeted outreach
- Engaging voluntary organizations to help augment resources for public safety, preparedness and response capabilities
- Integrating the whole community and integrating nontraditional resources to ensure disaster preparedness."[55]

At Ready.gov there are resources to begin a Citizen Corps Council that brings together local government, business, and community leaders who work to prepare their communities for disaster and make them more resilient. There are also programs for youth preparedness and annual **"Prepareathon" events** that give residents a chance to practice what to do during an emergency. "This practical, hands-on exposure helps build more confident, better prepared individuals and communities."[56]

One of the most critical issues in acute readiness for your community will be **community communication**. Libraries that invest in building a strong social media following, which publish community

---

55. https://www.ready.gov/citizen-corps.
56. https://www.ready.gov/prepareathon.

newsletters that feature information not just about the library but about the community at large, and which even use radio programming will be better positioned to help get the word out in the aftermath of a disaster, as well as build long-term resiliency in their communities. Leveraging our following in these markets to get out the word, not just about library programs and services, but about public service announcements as well, will build the library's stature as a community information hub, and this could be absolutely critical in the event of an acute disruption in the community. Another essential part of a strong communication strategy for the future will be ready access to municipal and "siren services" leadership: fire, police, and emergency medical services. The leadership of the library should cultivate, if not begin, a Community Resilience e-mail or text list so that a relationship with key stakeholders has been established *before* an acute disaster strikes. Leveraging online collaboration tools like Dropbox, Google Drive, and Slack to cultivate these leadership networks could be a smart role for the library to play.

LONG-TERM READINESS: INSIDE YOUR LIBRARY

Librarians are long-haul thinkers. By our very calling we focus on preservation—of access, of information. We focus on lifelong learning, and we invest time, resources, and energy in educating people of all ages because we believe in their future, we want them to succeed, to go on and do good. We are the epitome of paying it forward. We are consistently thinking about how to assist our community in the face of mounting challenges and disruptions, whether they be technological, economic, or societal. However, there is much work to be done related to our own operations to ensure long-term readiness for the future.

In the area of staff training, there should be a concerted effort to increase the **ecological literacy** of library staff. As staff make decisions, plan programs, purchase items, and decide how to best allocate the library's time, space, and funds, they will better understand what it will take for their local and global community to be sustainable and resilient, and the better our chances are to embed the necessary eco-ethic into our services, programs, outreach, and partnerships. No one person in an organization can create the necessary momentum we will need for libraries to make a dent in the issues facing our communities; this is something that calls for **all hands on deck**. Ecological literacy skills should be part of job training, job descriptions, and job evaluations—from the custodian to the director, there are choices made every day that could be improved with this lens through which to view the world. For a deeper dive on this issue, check out the book *Sustainable Thinking* from the American Library Association.

Libraries should overtly demonstrate a commitment to **equity, diversity, and inclusion** in their operational practices, from the hiring of staff to board recruitment to programming and collection development. A calling card of every library needs to be a reflection of diverse perspectives. If we do not reflect the world around us, we cannot maximize our appeal to a broad cross-section of our local community, or truly call ourselves educators. This is key to the trust necessary to play an important role in building a community's resilience.

Libraries should promote **creative problem-solving** both inside the library and in the community. From employing design thinking—an iterative, flexible, and collaboration-focused process to find solutions to shared problems—to offering seed grants that can bring good ideas to life in the community, **libraries can be incubators for tomorrow's solutions**. This can be applied in a focused endeavor, like the Madison

Public Library's Library Takeover program, or through workplace challenges that enable staff to identify, ideate, prototype, and test theories on a faster cycle than traditional library planning allows for.

Libraries can approach resilience holistically by using new certification programs that hold great promise for the future resilience of libraries and the contributions that libraries can make to more resilient communities.

The **New York Library Association** recently launched a **Sustainable Library Certification Program** to help public libraries work through the various aspects of embedding sustainability in their library and better position themselves as community leaders. The program seeks to provide a certification path for libraries in the same way that the U.S. Green Building Council's Leadership in Energy and Environmental Design (LEED) program does for buildings and B Corp does for business practices. To achieve the certification, libraries will engage in the following activities:

- Data collection and benchmarking so libraries can track their success as they progress through the program
- Policy writing to institutionalize best practices as a sustainable library
- Program and partnership development with an eye toward the sustainability of the library's community

All of the program's activities are designed to help libraries position themselves as **sustainability leaders in their community**. There are twelve categories in all: seven environmental-centric categories (e.g., energy, waste, water) and five library-centric categories (e.g., community involvement, social equity and resiliency, financial sustainability, collections). All of these add up to helping libraries **improve their triple bottom line as environmental stewards, economically feasible institutions, and institutions that place great stock in social equity**. Coming soon is a similar tool for school and academic libraries.

The **RELi Collaborative** has provided the **RELi Rating System**. RELi (pronounced "rely") provides a structure for designing buildings and communities that are "shock resistant, healthy, adaptable and regenerative through a combination of diversity, foresight and the capacity for self-organization and learning."[57] This rating system provides a checklist of planning, design, engineering, and operating actions to make a local project and the world at large more resilient. In very big news, the U.S. Green Building Council has announced the adoption of RELi.

Facility planning provides a wealth of opportunities for libraries to better prepare and respond with resilience. Libraries with new construction and major expansion and renovation opportunities have lots of guidance on how to build in more resilience thanks to LEED, the Living Building Challenge, and RELi. But for libraries with modest facility plans in the future, one major focus should be on **energy independence**. Retrofitting facilities with solar or other renewable energy sources so that the library can still operate when the electrical grid goes down should be a goal of every library in the world. Libraries are already one of the smartest organizations in our communities, and their facilities should be too. Other priorities we should be seeing in library master facility plans should include maximizing large and small **meeting spaces**, cultivating **outdoor spaces** for interaction and learning, and **wireless mesh networks** that extend as far into your service area and beyond your facility as possible. Future library spaces—indoors and out—need to be about **people**, not stuff.

---

57. http://c3livingdesign.org/?page_id=5110.

Micro-grids and community solar are emerging trends that libraries should have on their radar. Micro-grids are "localized grids that can disconnect from the traditional [electrical] grid to operate autonomously. . . . and help mitigate grid disturbances to strengthen grid resilience."[58] Community solar involves solar-electric systems that provide power to, or are owned by, multiple community members. A 2008 study by the National Renewable Energy Laboratory found that only 22–27 percent of residential rooftop area is suitable for housing an on-site solar photovoltaic system. Community-centric options are necessary to expand access to solar power.[59] Libraries are all about access, so why not help provide access to yet another essential service, electricity?

Particularly in areas of the world plagued by drought, **net zero water** buildings (constructed or renovated) will be the wave of the future. These buildings are designed to minimize total water consumption, maximize alternative water sources, minimize wastewater discharge from the building, and return water to the original water source.[60] The goal of net zero water is to preserve the quantity and quality of natural water resources with minimal deterioration, depletion, and rerouting of water.

Libraries should take their role of **preserving access to information**—from local history to climate change data—extremely seriously. A hard look at where unique data lives and who preserves access to it will be key in an **era of obfuscation.** Information is power, and no one knows that better than librarians. Presenting a political message that minimized or denied outright the human role in causing—and fixing—climate change was a lot easier to do prior to the widespread, published assent among scientists, the cohesive reports from the UN Intergovernmental Panel on Climate Change, and the indisputable data coming from

58. https://www.energy.gov/oe/activities/technology-development/grid-modernization-and-smart-grid/role -microgrids-helping.
59. https://www.nrel.gov/docs/fy11osti/49930.pdf.
60. https://www.nrel.gov/docs/fy16osti/65298.pdf.

the National Aeronautics and Space Administration (NASA) and the National Oceanic and Atmospheric Administration (NOAA). But what if data about climate change were to be suppressed? What if it were no longer accessible via government websites or, worse, no longer collected owing to a loss of funding for earth science research, if not outright bans on that research? Would political forces then revert to economically and politically driven decisions that don't put the health and well-being of our planet and the humans who inhabit it first?

As the U.S. presidential inauguration approached in January 2017, a story caught my eye about a "Guerilla Archiving" event at the University of Toronto. This hackathon was targeting the preservation and archiving of climate and environmental data from the Environmental Protection Agency and the NOAA. Then another story popped up about a similar event at the University of California, Los Angeles, and there were subsequent stories about librarians, archivists, and programmers banding together to do similar work at events such as DataRescue Philly at the University of Pennsylvania and the Internet Archive's Gov Data Hackathon in San Francisco.

Then *WIRED,* a mainstream publication that focuses on how emerging technologies affect culture, the economy, and politics, covered the story "Rogue Scientists Race to Save Climate Data from Trump," which has been shared more than 273,000 times via social media. Who were the heroes in this piece? Librarians.

That's where the librarians came in. In order to be used by future researchers—or possibly used to repopulate the data libraries of a future, more science-friendly administration—the data would have to be untainted by suspicions of meddling. So the data must be meticulously stored under a "secure chain of provenance."

That's what we do. We preserve accurate information. We ensure access. And now our work is rightfully recognized as **a critical component of the resistance**. We live in interesting times. Our role has never been more critical, both in the immediate and the long-term future.[61]

LONG-TERM READINESS: IN YOUR COMMUNITY

As described earlier in this book, libraries need to focus intensely on connecting with their community in order to deepen **understanding, empathy, and respect** among residents and create the level of social cohesion necessary to weather the literal and figurative storms on the horizon.

Devotion to a community's **civic health** will be the basis of community problem-solving in the future.

Local government administrators are concerned with the state of our civil society as public employees, and our elected officials confront the demons of racism, economic disparity, concentrated unemployment, alienation, and unequal access to quality education in many urban places. These factors may be smoldering or lay dormant in your community and unseen due to the economic and racial segregation that underlies the residential neighborhoods of many communities.

"Ferguson, Baltimore, and the Search for Civic Health Metrics," International City/County Management Association, August 2015[62]

61. Excerpted from my *Library Journal* article "Subversive Librarians," April 21, 2017.
62. https://icma.org/articles/ferguson-baltimore-and-search-civic-health-metrics.

Advocates of civic health have identified job creation, early childhood education, voter participation, parental involvement, civic engagement, crime and disease prevention, and higher levels of community connectivity as the building blocks of stronger communities.

In California, the City of Santa Monica has developed a Wellbeing Index,[63] creating a dimension framework to capture elements of wellbeing:

- **Outlook:** How do the people of Santa Monica feel about themselves and their lives?
- **Community:** How strong is the sense of community and connection? Three subdimensions were identified: strong local networks, civic engagement, and community identity.
- **Place & Planet:** Does the physical and social environment support and promote wellbeing? Three subdimensions were identified: mobility, quality and access, and pride and use of place.
- **Learning:** Do people have the opportunity to enrich their knowledge and skill sets across their lifespan? Three subdimensions were identified: learning status, access to enrichment opportunities, and learning behaviors.
- **Health:** How healthy is Santa Monica? Three subdimensions were identified: physical and mental health status, access to health promoting resources, and healthy behaviors.
- **Economic Opportunity:** Can a diverse population live and thrive in Santa Monica? Three subdimensions were identified: affordability, opportunity, and business diversity.

This effort in Santa Monica entails collecting data within these six elements, which drives community discussion about potential solutions,

---

63. https://wellbeing.smgov.net/about/wellbeing-index.

ongoing engagement with key stakeholders, translation of findings into the city's budget development, and goal-setting activities. A recent report on the index reported on strengths and opportunities:

- in each ZIP code of the city
- by race/ethnicity
- by gender

The Index provides a baseline for understanding what contributes to wellbeing and how the city and community can work to improve it. By understanding more about what makes us thrive, they can work together to make meaningful changes in their community. This is a comprehensive undertaking with extensive stakeholder buy-in and public/private investment. However, it is a trailblazing effort that can assist other municipalities in working together to strengthen their communities.

Libraries should be implementing tools such as the Public Library Association's **Project Outcome** to measure the efficacy of library programs and services in the areas of civic/community engagement, early childhood literacy, job skills, and economic development to ensure that what we think will work actually does work, and to adjust accordingly with the data we gather. The availability of outcome-based data will help libraries demonstrate how they contribute to a community's wellbeing.

Focusing in a holistic manner on the wellbeing of our communities may feel overwhelming to library leaders, but we do not need to wait for our municipalities to adopt a wellness mindset to be actively contributing to issues that impact all residents of our communities.

An example of an issue that is of concern to all residents is access to healthy food, particularly in areas of the country defined as "**food deserts**" where access to fresh fruit and vegetables and other healthy whole foods is becoming an issue of increasing concern. Some fear that the agricultural degradation already wrought in our world will disrupt the food supply and human health long before rising sea levels due to climate change will.[64] Communities that decentralize their food sources and grow diverse crops of fruits and vegetables closer to home will reduce costs for residents and build in resilience when food supply chains and transport routes are disrupted by climate change and severe weather. Libraries are already starting to lead the way on this issue, devoting land and rooftops to community gardens (see the Library Farm at the Northern Onondaga Public Library in New York, the South Sioux City Public Library in Nebraska, and the Rancho Cordova branch of the Sacramento Public Library in California) and hosting community-supported agriculture pickup points. Libraries that actively **incubate civic participation** will embody the idea of self-transcendence, helping others engage civically to benefit us all. What might this look like? Recent iterations of libraries that are focused on empowering citizens include:

- **Lexington Public Library** (Kentucky), which partnered with its community foundation, city government, chamber of commerce, public schools, and others to engage 11,000 citizens in a series of community conversations to inform the city's comprehensive plan
- **Kingston Library** (New York), which provides a "Civics Night School" program
- **Topeka & Shawnee County Library** (Kansas), which helps provide education for adults interested in running for elected office

The Johnson County Library's *Race Project KC* provides an excellent example of a library that is putting history to work for the future success of their community. *Race Project KC* is an annual immersive racial

---

64. https://www.theguardian.com/commentisfree/2017/oct/20/insectageddon-farming-catastrophe
    -climate-breakdown-insect-populations.

justice initiative focused on the history of the United States. Designed for students, grades 9 through 12, in the Kansas City metropolitan area, the program offers an investigation into the history of racial politics in Kansas City, the county, its schools, and how these issues affect us today. The vision of the project is "To empower students and teachers with the tools to understand our city and its peoples' past, critique the present, and build for a better future through dialogue and critical literacy. Students are active participants in their schools and communities, not just passive observers."[65]

Key to these examples is the *action orientation* of their work. These are not passive programs, but empowering events that are designed to stimulate **active participation** in civic life.

---

65. https://www.raceprojectkc.com/about.html.

CONCLUSION

LIBRARIANS ARE NOT JUST EDUCATORS BUT ACTIVISTS.
Libraries themselves are radical institutions that advocate and provide equal and open access for all. We must embrace the proactive nature of our work and reject timidity in the face of violence, oppression, and environmental devastation. We must fight for those we serve to ensure they have a chance at education, at life, at happiness. **This is not easy work.** This is a long-term commitment to the resilience of society.

Libraries and their leaders can be the example that sets the tone. Our facilities can be the model, and our policies, practices, and efforts can lead the way. So much of what libraries do is already helping communities go in the right direction, but libraries are seldom recognized for this. We need to **be bold**. Go for the big ideas, seek out third-party certification of our work, apply for awards that recognize our good work, and get over the chronic humility that afflicts the library profession. Leaders lead from the front, and to do that sometimes you need to **build your own front to lead from**. Don't wait for an invitation to step up; your community is counting on you.